Praise for *Embracing Diversity*

"What a gift and a challenge this book is. I have been challenged and blessed to walk with these pastors and teachers as their bishop. Now you can experience their vision that we as Christians and as Americans might live with joy a life in which we engage the work of racial reconciliation and the joy of living in relationship with people of many faiths and cultures. They will broaden and deepen your imagination and action as you embrace your vocation to love your neighbors with no exception."

—Jon Anderson, former bishop,
Southwestern Minnesota Synod, ELCA

"It is indeed time to embrace, not fear, the growing racial and religious diversity in America. This timely, challenging, and well-written book calls all of us to take seriously the gospel message to love our neighbors, without exception. The authors, deeply experienced in both interracial and interreligious dialogue and actions, provide excellent guidance for congregations and communities to mobilize to help America fulfill its promises of equity, opportunity, and justice."

—Serene Jones, President, Union Theological Seminary

"This book will inspire you to welcome the racial and religious diversity of twenty-first-century America. Moreover, it will provide you with the frameworks and skills necessary to help our nation become a thriving pluralistic democracy—the first ever in human history."

—Eboo Patel, founder, Interfaith Youth Core

"A clarion call to Christians to fight racism, to stand with our sisters and brothers of other faiths, to love the diversity that makes up our nation, and to take action before those who would do harm to the United States can succeed in destroying our country. This is an urgent message in a moment of crisis."

—Jim Winkler, president and general secretary,
National Council of Churches

Embracing Diversity

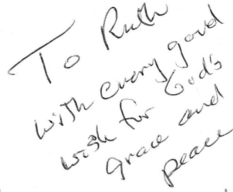

To Ruth
with every good
wish for God's
grace and
peace

Darrell Jodock
Bill Nelsen

Embracing
DIVERSITY

Faith, Vocation,
and the
Promise of America

Darrell Jodock
and
William Nelsen

FORTRESS PRESS
MINNEAPOLIS

EMBRACING DIVERSITY
Faith, Vocation, and the Promise of America

Copyright © 2021 Fortress Press, an imprint of 1517 Media. All rights
reserved. Except for brief quotations in critical articles or reviews, no
part of this book may be reproduced in any manner without prior written
permission from the publisher. Email copyright@1517.media or write to
Permissions, Fortress Press, PO Box 1209, Minneapolis, MN 55440-1209.

Scripture quotations are from New Revised Standard Version Bible,
copyright © 1989 National Council of the Churches of Christ in the United
States of America. Used by permission. All rights reserved worldwide.

Cover image: © Adobe Stock 2021; Black History by freshidea
Cover design: Alisha Lofgren

Print ISBN: 978-1-5064-7159-4
eBook ISBN: 978-1-5064-7160-0

Contents

Preface

Why this book? It is our call for fellow humans to embrace religious and racial diversity, not to fear it. It is our call for fellow Christians to love our neighbors more boldly and completely, not to limit that love. It is our call for people at all levels of our society, especially in our congregations and local communities, to speak out and take action, not to remain silent and inactive.

We are alarmed at how differently our society treats people of color. The tragic killing of George Floyd by a police officer in our home state of Minnesota and similar events around the nation have highlighted vividly this mistreatment of people of color in our policing and justice systems. The Covid-19 pandemic has made manifest in stark terms the long-standing disparities in the health care systems, housing conditions, educational opportunities, and economic outcomes among communities of color.

We are alarmed by the rise in overtly hostile acts directed at Jews, Muslims, Hindus, Buddhists, Sikhs, and sometimes Christians. These actions threaten to undermine the freedom of religion guaranteed by the Bill of Rights.

Wherein lies our hope for real and lasting change and the embracing of diversity in our country? We are convinced that the Christian message, when understood as a message of God's unconditional grace and love and a call for humans to pass that grace and love on to others, can help overcome the mistreatment of people in other religions and of other races. And the hope inspired by God's steadfast love can overcome the fears that feed injustice.

People of faith do not have all the answers and often make mistakes. But we are convinced that people of faith can be the catalyst for change, including the critical changes needed in structures, policies, and personal attitudes.

Why now? Because inaction will tear our society apart. Quick fixes will not work. Stoking fear will only make matters worse. The way forward involves seeking long-term solutions that reach the root of the problems.

Why combine these two topics—the interreligious and the interracial? In practice, the two intertwine. Muslim immigrants from Africa, for example, face both religious and racial barriers. The voices of white supremacy seek an America that is exclusively white and exclusively Christian. Both institutional racism and religious intolerance are dominant cultural influences.

In some ways, the solutions overlap. To build racial cooperation and improve interreligious relations, all of us need to cross over racial or religious boundaries in order to understand people on the other side. All of us need to treat others with dignity, cooperating with them for the common good, standing up for them in the face of antagonism, and standing with them in times of tragedy. Respect and inclusion are common goals for each endeavor.

That said, these two endeavors diverge in critical ways. Interreligious dialogue seeks ways to cooperate without ignoring the differences between one religion and another. In the experience of many, such engagement yields a deeper understanding and appreciation of one's own religion. Yes, it may affect the way a person interprets that religion, but it does not ask that one's own religion be abandoned.

Interracial understanding differs because it does ask white Americans to abandon elements of their typical outlook. For this to happen, they must listen and learn enough about how people of color are treated in order to begin to see themselves in a new way, as beneficiaries of racial privilege. If this process of gaining understanding and empathy works as it should, then people of color also begin to see themselves in a new way—as valued and trusted.

What can be helpful is to notice the direct parallel between the isolating and polarizing practices in the United States and the socioeconomic-political differences of the biblical world. Jesus associated with shepherds and fishermen, widows, and people without power or influence, and he challenged those political, religious, and economic leaders who ignored or mistreated them. What he was dealing with was structural injustice, not just individuals with problems.

Why these authors? We have sought to address these problems and offer ideas for action because we care deeply about the well-being of our society and about those who are excluded or hurt. We hope our experiences in race relations and interreligious dialogue can help illumine a way forward. We have both lived in different parts of the United States with religiously and racially diverse neighbors and in diverse neighborhoods. We have both spent our lives in higher education and in local parishes and know the power of good teaching. We draw from two relevant specialties: political science and religious studies/theology. We hope our collaboration can offer helpful insights for contemporary Christians and contemporary Americans.

But we are both white. Is there a place for white Christians to address interracial understanding? Yes is the answer we have received from others, including Black Christian authors. Why? Because moving beyond the structural racism and racist policies found in the United States requires that white Americans change their outlook and their behavior. For this real and lasting change to occur, counsel and encouragement from both fellow whites and people of color are required. Moreover, finding a compelling vision of an alternative takes deep engagement with the Scriptures. For all churches and Christians, the intersection of this biblical vision and a clearer perception of racial inequity is where movement toward racial justice can occur.

Our purpose in writing this book is to encourage individuals and faith communities to become engaged and to act—to reach across racial and religious boundaries in order to understand their neighbors and to commit themselves to stand with them and stand up for them. In so doing, we all will exercise our calling, our vocation as children of God, and our responsibility as citizens of this country.

Darrell Jodock and William Nelsen
St. Peter, Minnesota
June 29, 2021

Introduction

The Radical Call to Love Your Neighbor

On a beautiful sunny day in late August of 2017, thousands of people came to stand on the green grass or under the large trees on the Boston Common. Two groups of people with opposing views of the future of America were present that day, both exercising their constitutional rights to freedom of assembly and speech. One group, by far the smaller, had announced a rally to protest the increasing racial, ethnic, and religious diversity in America, calling for others to stand with them against cultural changes that would erode their view of the values of America. The announcement of their rally had prompted hundreds of congregational, civic, and neighborhood groups and thousands of individuals to respond in order to express a different view, a view that welcomed cultural diversity, tolerance, and respect for others as the true values of America. Many of those individuals or groups carried signs expressing their distaste for what they felt was "hate speech" or, more positively, expressing the need for "speaking out for justice" and "welcoming the stranger." But the sign that got the most attention was a large banner carried by a Methodist church group that read, "Love Thy Neighbor (No exceptions)."

Approximately one year later, eleven people were killed in a Jewish synagogue in Pittsburgh by an individual who over years had adopted destructive anti-immigrant and anti-Semitic beliefs. In the days that followed this terrible event, people gathered near the synagogue to express their sorrow for these deaths and to share their belief in the importance of an American culture that welcomed people of varying religious persuasions. Again, many people carried signs. But once more, one large banner carried by several individuals stood out. It read, "Love Thy Neighbor: No Exceptions!"

These words, "Love Thy Neighbor: No Exceptions," lie at the heart of the Christian message. The Hebrew Scriptures contain the charge to love the Lord your God with all your heart, soul, strength, and mind and a separate charge to love your neighbor as yourself (Deut 6:5; Lev 19:18). Jesus brought these together as the Great Commandment. And Jesus made it clear through the parable of the Good Samaritan and through his many other words and actions that "neighbor" carried an all-inclusive meaning.

Yet throughout history, including the history of America, many Christians have modified the meaning of "love thy neighbor" by interpreting it to mean "some neighbors." These Christians often screen out people of other colors, people who hold other religious beliefs or profess none, and people with political and social views that differ from theirs.

As Christians in an America struggling to accept our growing diversity, we can no longer define "loving your neighbor" in such a limited way. All Christians are called to love our neighbors in active, caring, and meaningful ways. And white Christians must recognize both our theological and our civic duty to define and love our neighbors much more radically, comprehensively, and actively.

When we say, "Love your neighbor without exception," what do we mean? We believe that the love described in the Gospels, and as seen in the actions of Jesus, is expressed in these visible and meaningful ways:

- Love is demonstrated by individual actions every day—such as saying hello to a stranger, sending a nice note or text, offering hospitality, or engaging in discussions with people of other races and faiths.

- Love is caring about the social, cultural, and structural circumstances of people who encounter discrimination and lack of opportunities because of the color of their skin or their religious beliefs.
- Love is learning to understand the beliefs, values, hopes, and problems of those neighbors who practice another religion or are shaped by different racial and cultural experiences.
- Love is caring that all people should have a chance to grow, learn, recover, and succeed.
- Love is working hard with others to change the laws, practices, structures, and public policies that hold people down.
- Love is being mobilized and mobilizing others to oppose the evils of our society.
- Love means moving away from old habits of inaction, including too readily accepting the status quo, refusing to reach out to others because of our ignorance and fear, refusing to act, and refusing to mobilize ourselves and others.
- Love means a willingness to share control, including with those who have been excluded from influence.
- Love removes the exceptions when answering the question "Who is my neighbor?"

When people look closely at this challenging list of love in action, they must readily admit that, as Christians, we have not lived up to the moral implications of the gospel message. We have not listened carefully to the good news that everyone is a creature of God and everyone is loved by God.

Likewise, as American citizens, we have not lived up to the promise of America. The Declaration of Independence and the Constitution are filled with language that calls for a nation of liberty and equality. And following years of violating those promises under slavery and Jim Crow laws, constitutional amendments and other laws made it clear that these ideals were meant to apply legally to all citizens of whatever color or creed. The promise of America is meant for all, not just the Anglo-Saxon forefathers who formulated and expressed the original American ideals.

Differences of race and religion have, from the beginning, been at the center of struggles to realize the American promise. Today these two—race and religion—have come together as powerful tests for our future. Many Americans live in fear of the not-so-distant time when white Americans will be in a minority and in fear that the privileges accorded the Christian religion will be lost when there are too many people of other faiths. Their view of America is still infused with the idea that "love your neighbor" is OK, as long as many designated exceptions are permitted.

We believe strongly that only with a broader and more radical understanding of the gospel message will Christians be able to embrace our racial and religious diversity, achieve justice for those who have been mistreated for so long, and finally, in cooperation with others, realize the true vision for our country. In the chapters that follow, we address the realistic challenges that confront us in bringing about needed changes. Yet we also seek to describe meaningful paths to help us all live out the call of the gospel message of unconditional love and the true promises of America. We seek to help people move from fear to faithfulness, from hate to hospitality, and from a journey in darkness to the joy of living in God's grace and God's diverse world.

The two of us are not entirely naive. We recognize that we are white Christians and white Americans. We see the world through the lens of our own economic, social, and racial standing, and we cannot pretend to understand fully what it is like to be a person of color. We have observed, but we have not had to deal, personally and day to day, with the racism that pervades our society. This racism is not primarily of the type that involves harassment or bodily injury. It is instead the pressure of social forces that cause experiences to differ so markedly among racial groups. This type of racism produces the absence of support systems and educational and employment opportunities. It includes policies and laws that are not equitable or not administered equitably. As white persons, what we can do is listen carefully, invite others to recognize the nature of the problem, and then work actively to change the patterns and policies that benefit some (including ourselves) while disadvantaging others.

Indeed, as white Christians and white Americans, we challenge ourselves and our white brothers and sisters to move forward courageously and lovingly to embrace diversity. And we urge our brothers and sisters of all races and religions to envision and work toward positive societal change rather than fear and resist it.

We also recognize that our nation has many challenges to overcome to move toward embracing our growing diversity. Faith can play a powerful role in making this happen. Yet the nature of faith is often misunderstood, and faith is often misused by people seeking political power, social control, or individual gains. Faith has often been mixed too closely with America's "civil religion" (the idea that America receives special blessings from God that give it special privileges and a unique status as the "light to the nations") that blesses the status quo instead of allowing the power of the gospel to inspire needed changes in legal and social structures. People have often also misunderstood the nature of race and the ways in which racial discrimination still enters into both individual lives and the social, political, and economic realms of our country. These critical issues must be addressed.

Recent events have made abundantly clear the need for critical changes in our society. The Covid-19 virus impacted communities of color much more harshly as a result of long-standing public health disadvantages. Asian Americans experienced discrimination and harassment as a result of unwarranted blame. Cries of "Black Lives Matter" arose again throughout the nation as a result of the senseless deaths of Black men and women, sparking peaceful protests but also anger and violence. These events, in addition to the frequent misuse of social media and the difficulties of a severely divided citizenry, have set forth major tests for this nation. Will its people be able to move beyond division to dialogue? From self-centeredness to community building? From silence to action? If not, none of us will realize the hope of the gospel message or the promise of America.

Where do we turn for special help and understanding in order to move forward? We are convinced that often overlooked is a proper understanding of the concept of Christian vocation—a calling from God—that should play a much more prominent role in our daily individual and communal lives. Understanding one's vocation can be vital to embracing diversity in this nation; it leads people to recognize that they are called to move from self-interest to seeing the needs of others, to reach out in hospitality and love, to be actively engaged in healthy dialogue across religious and racial boundaries, to join with others to bring about much needed structural and economic changes in our society, and to live in realistic hope for a new day of reconciliation and fellowship with our neighbors of all colors and faiths.

Finally, we want to make it clear that we are two persons who believe in the power of the Christian faith for good, despite the mistakes and flaws that the institutional church and its believers have evidenced over the years. In fact, given the current political divisiveness, we believe that the Christian church—Protestant and Catholic—is called to take the lead in moving this nation toward the embrace of diversity. We also believe that the best way to do this is in collaboration with those of other faiths, as we all live together and work together for the common good.

The time is now. The time is now for the people of our congregations to embrace religious and racial diversity. The time is now to move past a fear of change and a tolerance of old habits and structures that prevent change. The time is now for congregations and communities to mobilize to embody the message of the gospel and the promises of our nation. The time is now to realize the high calling of our Christian vocation—this year, this month, this day. The time is now to move from resolutions and words to action. The time is now to love our neighbors without exception! Let's get started.

CHAPTER ONE

A Nation of Diversity
To Fear or Embrace?

RACIAL DIVERSITY:
FROM MELTING POT TO MOSAIC

When we were growing up in the Midwest and Northwest parts of the country in the 1950s, we were taught in school that America served as a great example to the world because the United States represented a "melting pot" for people from various nations. Indeed, we felt a special sense of pride in believing that we were part of a welcoming, tolerant nation, clearly better in this respect than other nations around the globe.

Yet as we grew in understanding of the larger cultural scenes throughout our country, we realized that there were significant restrictions on how much "melting" was really occurring and who could actually be welcomed into the "pot." Segregation of Blacks and whites was still supported by Jim Crow laws in the South and by neighborhood dividing lines and "redlining" housing practices in northern cities. The nature of immigration was changing. Although some time had been required for our grandparents, who came from places like Norway, Denmark, and Scotland, to become accepted and to adjust to the practices of their new country, it was easier to envision people from various European nations entering the cultural mix of America than immigrants from other parts of the world. Immigrants were expected not only to pledge allegiance to the United States' way of governing but also to adopt the cultural norms of the majority. Diversity was present but not written large in most northern states and cities.

Today, the idea of a "melting pot" is even less accurate than when we first heard it. Our racial and religious diversity is more visible. *Mosaic* may be a much better term for describing the current and future American landscape.

And this "true diversity" will continue to become more prominent in America in the coming decades. The noted demographer William H. Frey has described the current realities, the expected trends, and their profound impact in his recent book *Diversity Explosion*. He notes these important changes: In 2011, "for the first time in the history of the country, more minority babies than white babies were born in a year."[1] When the 2020 census is complete, it "is expected to show that two-fifths of the nation's population identifies itself with a racial group other than white."[2] Then within another two decades, America will become truly a mosaic landscape: "Sometime after 2040, there will be no racial majority in the country."[3] There will also be a much larger number of people who are themselves multiracial, as multiracial marriages continue to grow.

A person could assume that this continuing increase in diversity will result from increased immigration from other countries. Not so! As Frey points out, "This growth in diversity will occur irrespective of shifts in immigration levels."[4]

Residential segregation, especially Black-white segregation, still exists in many areas of the country, especially in the large northern cities. Yet this pattern is also changing as more Blacks enter the middle class and move to the suburbs. Blacks are also reversing the old movement to the North as many relocate to new economic opportunities in southern states.

The largest minority growth is occurring among Hispanics and Asians. Frey points out that "between 2015 and 2060, Hispanics and Asians will roughly double in size, and the multi-racial population will triple."[5]

What about rural communities that have often been more isolated from diversity trends? This part of our landscape will also change significantly, as people of color from various backgrounds fill jobs currently held by older whites who will be retiring. Many minority families will continue to move to rural and small-town areas where costs are lower than in the big cities.

This growth in diversity will have a significant impact on all Americans. Perhaps the most powerful and meaningful change will be the creation of what Frey describes as the "cultural generation gap,"[6] a gap between the increasingly diverse youth population and the older population that will still be mostly white.

This generation gap, along with the overall changes in minority populations, will require all Americans to make adjustments to benefit all groups. "Loving your neighbor as yourself" will mean that older Americans will need to support education, job growth, and affordable housing for younger, diverse Americans. In turn, the support of younger Americans will allow the nation to maintain Social Security, Medicare, and other critical programs for senior citizens. And to maintain a strong economic situation for all Americans, both political parties—Republican and Democratic—will need to increasingly move across color lines. Republicans will need to reach out to people of color, and Democrats will need to appeal to more of this increasingly older white population.

RELIGIOUS DIVERSITY:
FROM ONE RELIGION TO PLURALISM

The religious landscape of America is also changing, and it has been changing for the last several decades. For much of our history, America was thought to be a "Christian nation," and in the minds of many during most of the first two hundred years, this meant a "Protestant nation." That image began to change as Catholics moved into the political spotlight from the time of Al Smith's presidential candidacy in 1928 to John F. Kennedy's victory in 1960. At the same time, after World War II, Americans began recognizing the importance of Christianity's strong link to the Hebrew Bible and the Jewish faith and increasingly described ourselves as a nation founded on Judeo-Christian principles.

Yet extensive research by the Pew Research Center in 2007 and 2014 reveals a different picture concerning our religious mix.[7] Protestants no longer constitute a majority of US adults (46.5 percent in 2014 vs. 51.3 percent in 2007). Overall, however, individuals of the Christian faith still dominate the American religious scene. Pew's research indicated that 70 percent of Americans still identified with some denomination of Christianity. At the same time, the most striking change from 2007 to 2014 was the increase in the number of people who are religiously unaffiliated, from 16 percent in 2007 to 23 percent in 2014. These Americans are often labeled the "nones."* More recent Pew surveys indicate that these trends continue. Pew telephone surveys in 2018 and 2019 show that 65 percent of Americans described themselves as Christian and 26 percent as "religious unaffiliated."[8]

The percentage of Americans who identify with non-Christian faiths also increased from 4.7 percent in 2007 to 5.9 percent in 2014. Growth was more prominent among Muslims and Hindus. Yet it should be noted that the overall percentages of people in non-Christian faiths are fairly small and growing at a modest rate. (Population percentages for the largest non-Christian faiths in 2014 were Jewish, 1.9 percent; Muslim, 0.9 percent; Buddhist, 0.7 percent; and Hindu, 0.7 percent.)

---

* It is hard to determine how much the increase in the number of "nones" reflects changes in church participation or how much it is simply more socially acceptable to be "unaffiliated." In the past, the number of people who told pollsters that they were "Presbyterian" or "Methodist" or "Catholic" or some other denomination has always been larger than the number of persons who were actually members of these churches. Some considered it important to claim a connection, even if they were not members and not active in a congregation.

Immigration has had an impact on our religious mix, although not as much as many Americans might assume. Two-thirds of the immigrants coming to America from 2007 to 2014 were Christians. About one in ten of the total immigrants identified themselves as non-Christian.

As is the case with our American racial mix, intermarriage is having an important impact on our diversity. Pew's research indicates that almost 40 percent of Americans who have joined in matrimony since 2010 are in denominationally or religiously mixed marriages, in contrast with less than 20 percent of those who married before 1960. Racial diversity and religious diversity are increasingly merging as parts of the same overall American scene. Even members of churches that are still predominantly white or all-white see reports that their denominations are changing nationwide. Pew research reports indicate that racial and ethnic minorities now make up 41 percent of Catholics, 24 percent of evangelical Protestants, and 14 percent of mainline Protestants, with all those figures representing significant increases over previous decades. There is also a wide range of ethnic and racial diversity within several of the non-Christian faiths. Muslim American Eboo Patel in his book *Out of Many Faiths* reports that Muslims living in the United States come from seventy-seven different countries and that Muslims are the "only faith community in the United States with no majority race."[9]

How do we describe this current American religious scene? While we have noted that the term *mosaic* can be used to describe our current and growing racial mix, some leading commentators on our multireligious growth have suggested the term *pluralism* as a better descriptor. Diana Eck of Harvard Divinity School sees "pluralism" as more than diversity. It includes people of diverse religious identities living and working together for the benefit of their neighborhoods. Patel expands the definition of pluralism into "an ethic that has three parts: respect for different identities, relationships between diverse communities, and a commitment to the common good."[10]

Despite all the changes described above, America remains a nation of millions of religious believers and can likely be described as the most devout among nations in the Western world. And whether Americans describe themselves as a "mosaic" or as a nation of "pluralism," it is indeed the most religiously and racially diverse country in the world. Thus the questions for each of us Americans are these: Will we embrace this diversity, or will we fear it and oppose it (either directly or in more subtle ways)? Will we see this situation as a unique opportunity to show the rest of the world that people of varying races and religions can not only live together but also work together to advance the common good? Will our denominations at the national level and, perhaps most importantly, our churches at the local level be bold and courageous leaders in bringing us together to care for each other and join in mutual work and service? Will we love our neighbors without exception?

CHAPTER TWO

The Meaning of Faith for Embracing Diversity

Religious concepts can have different meanings for theologians and for people in congregational pews. Confusion can result. In order to understand more fully the claims and ideas expressed in the sections and chapters that follow, we seek first to clarify several often-used religious concepts. Especially important are the meanings embedded in the words *faith, religion,* and *spirituality.* How these words are defined and used has critical implications for addressing issues of religious and racial diversity along with the urgent need our society faces for civil discourse, social change, justice, and peace.

FAITH IS RELATIONAL AND SELF-INVOLVING

Accepting the truth of a proposition, such as "the earth goes around the sun," may not commit a person to any kind of loyalty or behavior. For most of our everyday activities, accepting this scientific truth will not make much difference. But at its most basic level, faith is relational and self-involving. It is best understood as a deep trust. A very old story tells of a tightrope walker who performed remarkable stunts on a high wire strung over Niagara Falls. He returned to the shore and asked a spectator, "Do you believe I can push this wheel-barrow on the wire all the way across the Falls?" The spectator, who had been very impressed with the performance, said, "Yes, sure." The tightrope walker responded, "Then get into the wheelbarrow." Faith is relational and self-involving. It's like trusting another enough to get into the wheelbarrow. Religious faith is a deep trust in God.

FAITH IS ALSO A RESPONSE TO GENEROSITY

Why should we trust someone? It is because they have shown us some kind of generosity. They have treated us well or have stood with us when things were tough or have taken our talents seriously and encouraged their development. The Gospels introduce us to the generosity of Jesus, who readily responds to people in need—be it a need for food or for health or for hope—and then claim "God is like this." Religious faith is a response to God's generosity. When a grandfather holds his hands out to his two-year-old granddaughter and encourages her to jump, she does so, not because she under-stands the concept of trust or can explain it, but because she has experienced her grandfather (and other family members) as loving and trustworthy. The same is true of God. When we humans expe-rience God as loving, generous, and trustworthy, the first response generated is one of acknowledging this love and generosity. Over time, this acknowledging grows into trust. Not to respond to God's generosity is to go on living as if that generosity did not exist, try-ing to "go it alone." When divine love begins to melt the barriers we ourselves have established, then faith takes root and grows. Faith is a relational, self-involving response to the good news of God's grace and our own experiences with the divine.

How do the gifts of love and generosity come to us? They come through other creatures and other people—through parents, teachers, mentors, neighbors, pastors, caring school boards, well-functioning governments, and others too numerous to mention. Our lives have been formed and shaped by the love and generosity and assistance of others. Faith recognizes God as the ultimate source of these gifts, even when they come through the words and deeds of those around us. A faith built on unmerited divine generosity will not be manipulative.

Any relationship of trust between one human and another is also built on generosity. If white folks and people of color are to establish healthy relationships or if Christians and Muslims are to do so, the first step is one of generosity—either on our part or on the part of the other. (Once the relationship matures, of course, we can expect some form of mutual generosity to be practiced.)

FAITH INSPIRES HOPE

Again and again, frightened people in the biblical story hear these words from God: "Fear not, for I am with you." A trustworthy God will still be there in the future. This promise can overcome fear. And this promise can inspire hope. Because of our vulnerability as humans, overcoming fear and inspiring hope can be important at any time, but they are especially important in the face of significant societal and cultural changes. Since the industrial revolution of the eighteenth and nineteenth centuries, our society has assumed that abundant natural resources could sustain limitless industrial growth, but now this can no longer be assumed; our level of consumption is not sustainable. We're dealing with a basic change with unknown consequences. Likewise, for four hundred years, whites have been the majority in the United States, but that is soon to change as whites become a minority among minorities. The adjustments required are frightening to many. Hope allows us to face them rather than blame others for them or try to run from them into defensive isolation.

FAITH AND UNDERSTANDING ARE NOT THE SAME

It is important to distinguish between faith, which is relational, and one's understanding of faith, which is more conceptual. Faith is faith, but a person's understanding of that faith can change and grow. A good analogy comes from our relationship with a loving parent. When we are eight years old, a parent may seem ideal—our hero. But when we are thirteen or fourteen, the same person may seem arbitrary and "old fashioned." By the time we are twenty, we begin to perceive our parent's complexity—a mixture of sterling qualities and individual quirks, or competencies and limitations. (Mark Twain once remarked that when he was fourteen, his father didn't understand anything. By the time he was twenty-one, he was surprised how much his father had learned in seven years!) These changes in understanding do not threaten the solidity of the parent-child relationship, anchored as it is in the reliability of the parent's love. The relationship is not the same thing as one's understanding of it.

What this means is that faith can be aided by reason and knowledge, but it is not a product of reason or knowledge. It is built primarily on a relationship of trust. Trust is a response to the perceived trustworthiness and graciousness of the other. Where increased knowledge becomes important is in guiding the outcome of this faith. Understanding God's purpose for the world influences a person's decisions regarding what to do and why. Understanding one's neighbor informs how to treat that person. And understanding how a community works guides a person's civic involvement.

When we who take our religion seriously understand that faith is a relationship of trust and that we arrive at faith by grace, we can be more open to people who hold different religious beliefs than we do, recognizing that they also arrived at their faith relationship in a similar manner.

FAITH INVOLVES SHARED PRIORITIES

In matters of religion (and in many other matters), to have faith in another is to accept that person's vision of what should be. In the Gospel of Luke, chapter 4, Jesus begins his ministry in his hometown of Nazareth. He attends the synagogue and reads from the scroll of Isaiah:

> The Spirit of the Lord is upon me,
>   because he has anointed me
>   to bring good news to the poor.
> He has sent me to proclaim release to the captives
>   and recovery of sight to the blind,
>   to let the oppressed go free,
> to proclaim the year of the Lord's favor. (Luke 4:18–19)

Then he sits down and says, "Today this scripture has been fulfilled in your hearing" (Luke 4:21).

To trust in Jesus is to sign on to this vision, to adopt these priorities, to enroll in the movement he has begun. The character of this movement can be seen, for example, in Matthew chapter 25, where Jesus commends those who give the hungry food, the naked clothing, and the thirsty something to drink, who welcome the stranger, visit the sick, and visit those in prison. To trust in Jesus is to make these priorities one's own. He invites us to turn our attention to those on the margins, those without power, those who are in need.

FAITH BRINGS FREEDOM

Faith frees us from societal expectations regarding, for example, what counts as success and what counts as national loyalty. And faith frees us for service to the other. The rescuers—who in Nazi Germany risked their lives and the lives of their families to hide a Jew, a Rom (Gypsy), or other intended victim—are a good example of this dual freedom. They were free from the barrage of propaganda to which they had been exposed since 1933. Contrary to those messages, they saw people of another religion or another nationality first and foremost as humans. This made them free for action—free to risk assisting those the Nazis regarded to be "subhuman" and slated for destruction. Their freedom involved a sense of agency—a sense that they could do something to help even if they weren't capable of solving the whole problem. And that "something" meant the difference between life and death for those they hid.

Their freedom had another dimension. What they faced was unprecedented. They had no guidebook to follow. They found amazingly creative ways to hide those targeted by the Nazis—ways that often put them out of step with their friends and neighbors who felt too trapped to act and simply went along with the Nazi program. For the sake of another, the rescuers were free to innovate, free to be out of step, and free even to have their own reputations damaged, if such damage was what it took to help their neighbors.

FAITH IS VOCATION PRODUCING

Ever since the Reformation, Christians have recognized that not only monks, nuns, and priests but every person of faith has a calling or a vocation. Our calling is to channel the gifts of God to others. Our calling involves the shared priorities of Luke 4 and Matthew 25. In addition to emphasizing the importance of building caring and loving relationships, the Christian faith issues a call to love God's world and all the human beings that inhabit it. The vocation/calling is to see oneself, not as isolated but as nested in communal ties, not as immune to the needs of others but drawn out by them into serving the neighbor and the community in all areas of life. Vocation passes along to others what has been received and joins the Jesus movement, working to heal the world. Jesus's "love your neighbor as yourself" is an invitation to affirm one's vocation.

The call is not just to serve individuals; it is also to serve and reform the larger community. This is so because individuals and communities are so closely intertwined with each other. The health of one affects the health of the other. As we were writing this chapter, we witnessed the actions of four police officers in Minneapolis that caused the death of George Floyd. The deep significance of this event lies in the fact that, as much as some would like to think otherwise, no part of the community can be healthy if people of color are treated differently from whites. No white person and no person of color can be whole if any part of the community is treated unjustly. Working for the common good is working for the benefit of all, especially those who have been excluded; doing so is part of our vocation as people of faith and as humans.

RELIGION AND SPIRITUALITY

The word *religion* is often used to refer to the varied belief systems throughout the world. When someone is asked, "What religion do you practice?" she or he may answer, "Christianity," "Judaism," "Islam," "Buddhism," "Hinduism," or another specific religious identification. Yet when asked to describe religion as a concept, we would say that it typically involves a sense of wonder or awe, a sense of gratitude, and a sense of connectedness (connectedness with the divine, with other humans, and with other creatures). A sense of wonder contrasts with any attempt to manipulate God or manipulate other humans and with any claim to have complete knowledge of God or the world. A sense of gratitude contrasts with any claim to be entitled to what we have. And a sense of connectedness contrasts with individualism—the view that a human can be whole and complete in isolation. A sense of connectedness inspires our sense of vocation. Some would label this threefold religious awareness "spirituality," but we do not agree with any attempt to separate "spirituality" from "religion" or to narrow "religion" to refer only to the institutional structures that are affiliated with faith communities. As we use the term, the heart of "religion" is this threefold sense of wonder, gratitude, and connectedness, even though each religion also includes its own distinctive practices and beliefs.

This basic religious orientation toward life gets expressed in quite different ways in the religions of the world; it is not unique to Christianity. Even if religions share a sense of awe, for example, this does not make them the same. They express it quite differently. The different ways of expressing and interpreting this awe are very significant because they shape different "ways of walking," or ways of living. An appreciation for both this underlying similarity and these significant differences means that we cannot say that all religions are the same nor that other religions are completely different. Nor should we claim that we believers have all the right answers to every possible religious question. Because God is God and we are not; we do not and cannot understand God fully. Such a complete understanding is simply not a human prerogative.

THE CHRISTIAN FAITH AND EMBRACING DIVERSITY

Given these clarifications of religious concepts, how does our specific Christian faith prepare us not only to live in an increasingly diverse society but actually to embrace this diversity and find meaning and joy in doing so?

At the heart of the Gospel story, Jesus's charge to us for a life well lived is straightforward: "You shall love the Lord your God with all your heart, and with all your soul, and with all your strength, and with all your mind; and your neighbor as yourself" (Luke 10:27). This is a call to trust and a call to vocation. In response to the question "Who is my neighbor?" in Luke 10:29, Jesus shares the Parable of the Good Samaritan, using the actions of an outsider to emphasize how "loving your neighbor" reaches far beyond family and friends and fellow members of a religion. The parable removes all limits from the call to care for and serve others.

This well-known parable has profound implications for how we relate to people of other religions and races. We know the parable well, but what often goes wrong is that we who have heard the message of God's love as proclaimed and lived by Jesus fail to grasp in our hearts and minds that the person of another religion or another race is also a neighbor. In Luke 10, Jesus is asked by a man "wanting to justify himself" (Luke 10:29)—that is, seeking to have Jesus draw a line between neighbor and nonneighbor—"Who is my neighbor?" Jesus replies with this parable. In it, the one who stops to help is a man the questioner and those in the audience regard to be an outsider. The travelers the audience considers to be "like us" walk by on the other side, but the Samaritan, who is not "like us," helps the man who has been beaten and robbed and left in a ditch. Jesus then returns to the questioner and asks him a different question: "Which of these three, do you think, was a neighbor to the man who fell into the hands of the robbers?" (Luke 10:36). He answers, "The one who showed him mercy." Jesus replies, "Go and do likewise" (Luke 10:37). The change in question is significant. Instead of drawing limits between who is or is not one's neighbor, Jesus shifts the question to who behaves as a neighbor. The limits are removed. The calling is to treat the person of another race and the person of another religion as a neighbor; no exceptions.

In an effort to communicate how jarring this parable was to Jesus's listeners, Clarence Jordan, a white biblical scholar and the founder of the integrated Koinonia Farm in Americus, Georgia, retold it in 1969 in his *Cotton Patch Version of Luke and Acts*:

A man was going from Atlanta to Albany [Georgia] and some gangsters held him up. When they had robbed him of his wallet and brand-new suit, they beat him up and drove off in his car, leaving him unconscious on the shoulder of the highway.

Now, it just happened that a white preacher was going down that same highway. When he saw the fellow, he stepped on the gas and went scooting by.

Shortly afterwards a white Gospel song leader came down the road, and when he saw what had happened, he too stepped on the gas.

Then a black man traveling that way came upon the fellow, and what he saw moved him to tears. He stopped and bound up his wounds as best he could, drew some water from his water-jug to wipe away the blood and then laid him on the back seat. [In a footnote, Jordan imagines the black man saying, "Yeah,

I know. They pass me by too."] He drove on into Albany and took him to the hospital and said to the nurse, "You take good care of this white man I found on the highway. Here's the only two dollars I got, but you all keep account of what he owes, and if he can't pay it, I'll settle up with you when I make pay-day."

Jesus then asks, "Now if you had been the man held up by the gangsters, which of these three—the white preacher, the white song leader, or the black man—would you consider to have been your neighbor?"[1]

The difference between Jesus's hearers and the Samaritans was religious. Jordan shifts the focus to race, but the shift from "Who is my neighbor?" to a redefinition of what it means to *be* a neighbor is the same.

We have described faith as built on generosity and as relational, self-involving, hope-inspiring, and vocation producing. And we have said that it brings deep freedom. Deep freedom is the kind found in a healthy relationship. It is not a self-serving, relationship-abandoning license. This deep freedom is free from coercion and free to focus attention on the other. It is free to listen and to serve the neighbor. It invites us to figure out how to serve the neighbor and the community. Yes, guidance from the Bible and the Christian tradition can be helpful, but the priority of faith-inspired behavior is not obeying a rule nor even safeguarding one's own virtue. What will benefit the neighbor is the highest consideration. The freedom that comes with faith is also the freedom to risk. In some cases, this risk can be relatively minor, as in reaching out to meet a person of another skin color or another religion and listening carefully, listening even when our ideas are challenged. In other circumstances, the risk can be much greater, as in stepping up to help someone who is being harassed or mistreated—whether by the police or by others.

In all these important ways, our Christian faith prepares us to love and serve our neighbors, to understand more completely who our neighbors are, and to embrace the growing diversity in our nation.

OUR CHRISTIAN FAITH AND RELIGIOUS INCLUSION

Religious faith is not to be confused with religious beliefs or with religious ideas. As we have emphasized, faith is relational. Beliefs are ideas that seek to describe that relationship. Trusting God is not the same as claiming that, for example, God is omnipotent. Not only are the two distinct, but specific beliefs—as we have seen—can change without destroying one's faith. Moreover, new experiences, including engaging with people of other religions and other racial, social, and economic backgrounds, can change a person's understanding of God and reshape one's beliefs without diminishing one's faith. Such encounters should not be feared.

It is also important to recognize that religion cannot answer every question. It is incomplete before our encounter with those who differ, and even if we learn a lot, it will be incomplete after that encounter. Christianity does not have all the answers! The book *Engaging Others, Knowing Ourselves* emphasizes that even devoted Christians are called to live with certain unanswered questions, such as "Why is there so much suffering in the world?" Persons of faith are called to reduce that suffering, not to explain it. Even the psalmists ask questions for which there are no answers, and Jesus says he does not know when the Son of Man will come (Mark 13:32). As Martin Luther insisted, God is simultaneously hidden and revealed. Revelation (primarily in and through the person of Christ) provides what we humans need to know about God, God's love, and God's vision for the world in order to sustain faith; but at the same time, God's hiddenness invites us to recognize the limits of our knowing—not just about God but also about ourselves and the world. Acknowledging these limits keeps us open to new wisdom and new discoveries—without compromising faith. Questions about ourselves, the world, and God are inexhaustible. Every new insight raises another question. No matter how much we know, there continues to be more to learn. The new questions we may face in dialogue with people in other religions "do not undermine our faith; faith is built on trust and does not have everything figured out."[2]

Christianity is not simply a set of belief statements or command-ments. It is basically a form of religious awareness—awareness of our relationship with God and with others and awareness of trust, wonder, gratitude, and our call to connect with and serve others. This religious awareness is not limited to Christianity. Wonder, gratitude, and con-nectedness get expressed in quite different ways in various religions, and we need to see this religious awareness in another religion before we can understand those who practice that religion. That is, we need to begin to understand the unique way religious awareness is expressed and lived out in that person's life. Despite the tendency of people in the United States to focus on the "beliefs" of a religion, beliefs are not a sufficient basis for understanding it. While looking at beliefs, it is too easy to miss the religious awareness from which everything springs and to miss the way it gets expressed in the day-to-day life of its adherents. Though the religions are distinctive, the presence of a basic religious awareness provides enough ground for cooperation. There is enough here to permit bridges to be built across the religious divides. (At least this is true so long as adherents do not misinterpret the nature of their own religion—as happens too often.)

Does an appreciation of another religion require that we reduce our commitment to our own faith? Not at all. Virtually always, what it does is deepen a person's commitment to and understanding of one's own faith. We come to see in our own religion things we may not have noticed and appreciate things about it that we took for granted. One's faith can be stronger when, after learning more about another religion, a believer makes an even more reflective commitment to the love and grace of Christ and the vocational pathway that such a commitment invites one to follow.

At the same time, learning more about another religion can help each of us understand and appreciate the values, similarities, and differences that arise from the religious journeys of those around us. Christians are still called to share the gospel, the good news of God's love for all, but we do so not by manipulating others, or ignoring them, or demeaning their religion, or failing to assist them in times of need. What is essential is caring for the dignity and well-being of every neighbor. Saint Francis of Assisi wisely stated, "Go out and preach the gospel. Use words if necessary."

We are reminded how C. S. Lewis, the Oxford Don and Cambridge professor, examined both reason and faith for the benefit of millions of people in his famous book *Mere Christianity* and his other writings. Reflecting on "What Christians Believe," he wrote, "I am going to begin by telling you one thing that Christians do not need to believe. If you are Christian, you do not need to believe that all other religions are simply wrong all through."[3]

Faith is relational. What this suggests is that we need to get to know how our neighbors in another religion experience their relationships with the divine. What claim does that relationship make on the way they interact with others and with the world? Just as there are diverse ways Christians understand and practice their faith, so there are diverse ways those in other religions understand and practice theirs. As helpful as it is to study and learn the basic teachings of another religion, it is even more important to come to know the people who practice it. We then can see that it is a way of life, not just a set of ideas to be endorsed or rejected.

Understanding the nature of faith opens the hearts and minds of believers to seek to understand, to engage with, and to love their neighbors of other religions, while at the same time strengthening and deepening their own commitments.

OUR CHRISTIAN FAITH AND RACIAL INCLUSION

How do we realize the potential of the Christian faith in relation to the growing racial diversity in America? Let us be honest. The history of Christianity in relation to enhancing race relations in our nation is, at best, a mixed bag. Christian slave owners on American plantations misused biblical passages that mentioned slavery to justify their ownership and treatment of slaves. At the same time, Christians, led by gospel messages, gave leadership to the abolitionist movement to end slavery. But denominational leaders, local clergy, and laypeople in many Southern churches gave strong backing to Jim Crow laws that enforced segregation and opposed equal opportunities for Black Americans. Even worse, for decades Christians failed to stand up against the lynching of Blacks, especially in the South. In Dr. James Cone's well-known book *The Cross and the Lynching Tree*, he wrote that between 1880 and 1940, "white Christians lynched nearly five thousand black men and women in a manner with obvious echoes of the Roman crucifixion of Jesus. Yet those Christians did not see the irony or contradiction in their actions."[4]

In the 1950s and 1960s, this "mixed bag" of Christianity's record concerning racial inclusion was again very evident in the public realm. The civil rights movement was led by Christians—not only by Rev. Martin Luther King Jr. and the Southern Christian Leadership Conference but also by thousands of Christian clergy and laypeople who joined the movement (along with many Jewish leaders and representatives of other faiths). Unfortunately, many other Christians opposed the movement, or stood on the sidelines, or felt that King and others were trying to move toward racial inclusion "too quickly."

The historical record shows that Christians often failed to oppose slavery. And the results are still with us. For both of these reasons, Christian churches and Christians as individuals are called now to engage actively in discussions and actions designed to promote interracial understanding, appreciation of our racial diversity, and mutual action for the common good. And most importantly, people of faith need to be active because the vision—of the gospel and of America—is still far from complete!

And just as we do in relation to religious diversity, we begin with the central gospel message of God's love and our vocation to love God, neighbor, and ourselves. We also remember the powerful words from Genesis 1:27 that "God created humankind in his image," thereby signaling that all people, of all racial identities, are made in God's image. All peoples in this colorful variety of our human landscape are our neighbors. God continues to reveal God's presence and purposes through the uniqueness and similarities of all people.

We earlier noted that personal faith is not diminished by active interchange and dialogue with people of other faiths. In the same way, an appreciation for one's own ethnic background is not lost by actively befriending and engaging with people of other races, learning about their backgrounds, and participating willingly and enthusiastically in a variety of their special customs. Humans are not called to be "color-blind," but to understand and appreciate their differences as well as their commonalities.

When Jesus said, "I was a stranger and you welcomed me" (Matt 25:35), he made clear to his disciples the importance of reaching out to people we may not have known well or known at all before, including those of other racial and ethnic backgrounds. And the apostle Paul followed his call to "love one another with mutual affection" (Rom 12:10) by reminding the Christians in Rome to "extend hospitality to strangers" (Rom 12:13).

By reaching out to people of other races and other faiths, we Americans no longer remain "strangers" but become acquaintances, friends, and active partners seeking mutual support, strengthening our communities and our nation. We all can continue to grow by loving our neighbors without exception.

CHAPTER THREE

Realizing the Promise of America for Embracing Diversity

THE CONSTITUTIONAL PROMISES

From the beginning of our nation, America's founders envisioned a nation that would be radically different from others in the way people had been treated and mistreated. This promise began with Jefferson's words in the Declaration of Independence: "We hold these truths to be self-evident, that all men are created equal, that they are endowed by their Creator with certain unalienable Rights, that among these are Life, Liberty and the pursuit of Happiness." These words laid the foundation for a democratic republic that would seek to allow people from various national, racial, and religious backgrounds to work together for the common good. As one historian has pointed out, even the words "pursuit of happiness" were meant to refer to "public happiness."[1]

The promise of America was embedded in the articles of the Constitution and its amendments, beginning with the preamble that spoke of forming a "more perfect Union," ensuring "domestic tranquility," promoting "the general welfare," and securing the "blessings of Liberty." To make the promise even stronger, the first ten amendments provided a bill of rights for all citizens that included a variety of personal protections and the freedoms of expression and religion.

Historians and independent commentators have often emphasized the uniqueness of these promises. The American political historian Arthur Schlesinger in his book *The Disuniting of America* described this distinctive vision as "America's creed": "The genius of America lies in its capacity to forge a single nation from peoples of remarkably diverse racial, religious (and) ethnic origins."[2]

The Swedish sociologist Gunnar Myrdal, while noting in 1944 that the United States had not realized its full promise to all people, especially African Americans, also referred to the "American Creed" that represented "devotion to principles of liberty, of self-government, equal opportunity regardless of race, gender, religion, or nation of origin."[3]

The American historian and biographer of Presidents Jefferson, Jackson, and George H. W. Bush, Jon Meacham, has gone even deeper when characterizing this nation's distinctive national promise using the words "the soul of America." The soul of America is expressed day-to-day by our leaders and by common citizens everywhere. To Meacham, the "dominant feature of that soul" is the belief expressed in the Declaration "that all men [persons] are created equal."[4]

Indeed, one can argue that the "soul of America" represents a civic expression of our calling to "love our neighbor" because that call, as we have seen, draws no lines and allows no exclusions. Everyone is our neighbor; all are created equal. When Americans more completely demonstrate their love of neighbors who represent the beautiful human diversity of our country, then we have a much greater chance of realizing the constitutional promises of our nation.

These promises still stand before us each and every day. We Americans learn them in our schools. We hear them often repeated, and we are reminded that our American experiment envisioned both racial and religious diversity, a diversity that promised freedom and equality for all.

THE PROMISE OF RACIAL EQUALITY:
A CHECKERED HISTORY

Yet any serious observer must readily admit that these promises, especially in America's failures to embrace racial diversity, have been very slow in coming, and in many ways are yet to be realized. As early as 1790, groups of citizens began to work to overcome the evils of slavery in America. The Pennsylvania Abolition Society and the New York Manumission Society joined with Black partners to seek Black freedom and equality.[5] William Lloyd Garrison founded the abolitionist newspaper *The Liberator* in 1831, and he and the noted Black author and speaker Frederick Douglass gave leadership to the movement in the decades prior to the Civil War.

Slavery in America was not ended until a series of important events occurred: the issuing of the Emancipation Proclamation by President Lincoln in 1863, a successful end to the Civil War in 1865, and the enactment of the Thirteenth Amendment later that year that formally outlawed slavery. The Fourteenth Amendment in 1868 was required in order to grant former slaves the right of citizenship and, at least "on paper," equal protection under the laws of the nation. Voting rights were given to Black men through the Fifteenth Amendment in 1870. These advances were short-lived, especially in the South, as the Reconstruction era was replaced by Jim Crow laws that enforced segregation and denied equal voting rights, educational opportunities, and access to public services. In the North, segregation and a lack of equal access to opportunities for African Americans were manifested by discriminatory housing regulations, local laws and policies, and more subtle prejudices. The formation of the NAACP in 1909 was one reaction to this failure of our nation to move toward the realization of America's promises.

Most Americans do not like to read the history of the dark years and racist activities of hate groups such as the Ku Klux Klan. The Klan, born after the Civil War to counter cultural changes in the South, was reborn following the release of the infamous movie *The Birth of a Nation* in 1915. In the 1920s, the Klan had chapters in all the forty-eight states and a membership estimated between two and five million. It supported white supremacist views not only against Blacks but against Catholics and Jews as well. Research by Jemar Tisby, writer for the *New York Times* and the *Atlantic* and a PhD student in history at the University of Mississippi, indicates that an estimated forty thousand Protestant ministers were members of the Klan during those years.[6] The widespread activities of the Klan decreased in the late 1920s because of opposition by national and local leaders, actions of the Supreme Court, and the writings of W. E. B. Du Bois and other advocates of racial equality. Unfortunately, the remaining Klan groups continued their violence long after the 1920s.

It took another four decades before the nation recognized that America's promise of racial equality was still significantly lacking. The civil rights movement, led by Rev. Martin Luther King Jr. and other church and civil activists, gave rise to to the Civil Rights Act of 1964 and the Voting Rights Act of 1965.

While the laws supporting segregation were changed because of the courageous leadership of King and others, the results of long-term government and private-sector structural racism have remained with us. Richard Rothstein has documented the legacy we see embedded in still segregated neighborhoods in his disturbing book *The Color of Law*, with the sad descriptive subtitle *A Forgotten History of How Our Government Segregated America*.[7] He describes how federal laws and practices prevented mortgage loans from being offered in racially mixed neighborhoods, how the GI Bill would not allow Black veterans to purchase homes in white communities, how private developers were subsidized to build large all-white suburban housing developments, and how local redlining and zoning practices reinforced the segregation that so many cities still witness today.

Another approach to maintaining residential segregation came through the placement of large public housing projects in designated Black neighborhoods. This practice occurred throughout various large American cities, but it was seen most vividly in Chicago, where

Mayor Richard J. Daley used giant public housing ghettoes to avoid Black movement into white neighborhoods.[8]

In the minds of many, the "victories" of the civil rights movement, as signified in new laws that outlawed local segregation ordinances and enhanced voting rights for all citizens, would surely and finally mean that all Americans would realize the nation's promises for equal treatment and opportunity. But sadly, this was not the outcome. Legal segregation may have ended, but racial prejudice, racial policies, and structural racism still persist. Racism shows up in the unequal sentences given to juvenile offenders. It shows up in the lower life expectancy for people of color and the lower levels of medical care for pregnant women of color. It shows up when whites react differently to Black teenagers walking down a street in their neighborhood than to a similar group of white youth. It shows up when voting is made more difficult in Black neighborhoods than in those that are predominantly white. Not only have some things not changed; others have gotten worse.

Other signs indicate that many Americans are reluctant to fully embrace racial and religious diversity. Interviews following the national election of 2016 revealed that many people felt alienated not only by a changing economy with fewer manufacturing jobs but also by visible racial and religious demographic changes and by the fear and uncertainties that social and economic changes always produce. These perceptions caused many to want to slow or reverse the changes they felt had impacted them negatively.

America's promises for racial equality have also been tested time and again by our immigration policies and the resulting arrival of new ethnic groups in our society. The promises to immigrants have been articulated well from our early years. In 1783, George Washington declared, "The bosom of America is open to receive not only the opulent and respectable stranger, but the oppressed and persecuted of all Nations and Religions."[9]

Theodore Roosevelt, a believer in the "melting pot" idea, was the first president to invite an African American into the White House when he welcomed Booker T. Washington and said in relation to immigrants, "A Scandinavian, a German, or an Irishman who has really become an American has a right to stand on exactly the same footing as any native-born citizen in the land."[10]

Throughout this nation's history, however, immigration has been limited in times of fear and uncertainty. In good times, newcomers have been welcomed, people have recognized the need to help immigrants, and they have acknowledged that more were needed for our economic growth. But at other times, our nation has reacted very negatively to opening its doors to immigrants.

For example, during President Chester Arthur's presidency, Congress passed the Chinese Exclusion Act out of fear that too many Chinese were competing for American jobs. The National Origins Act of 1924 set quotas for the number of immigrants and severely reduced the inflow. The nation reversed course following World War II, and in 1965, Congress passed the Immigration and Nationality Act that eliminated the national origins quotas from 1924 and paved the way to welcome more people from more countries. This change in policy resulted in a significant increase in our nation's racial diversity, with more nonwhite immigrants arriving from Asia, Africa, and Latin America.

This nation continues to struggle with two competing views regarding immigration that have been and continue to be prominent in our political and social scene. On the one hand, led by personal, humane, and spiritual concerns for the well-being of people suffering from violence and poverty in their home countries, many Americans have been prepared to welcome strangers in need of a better life. On the other hand, many political leaders have played on the fears of Americans that such immigrants will take away jobs, change our neighborhoods for the worse, or be "bad people" with criminal intent. The promise of America for immigrants will not be realized until the American people and our leaders can come together to forge a sensible, humane, and meaningful approach to immigration policy.

THE PROMISE OF RELIGIOUS EQUALITY: ESTABLISHMENT AND FREEDOM

The founders of our nation and those who drafted the words for the Constitution desired to create a society where a particular religious belief was not forced upon people by the ruling government. The search for religious freedom was a critical motivation for many people making the dangerous voyage to American soil.

This ardent desire for freedom of religious belief, expression, and worship was expressed in the First Amendment to the Constitution in two clauses in a single sentence: "Congress shall make no law respecting the establishment of religion, or prohibiting the free exercise thereof." Over the two centuries of our nation's existence, these words became known as "the establishment clause" and the "free exercise" or "freedom clause."

The establishment clause meant that the federal government could not adopt a particular religion and automatically make all citizens members of this chosen religion, as had been the case in several European nations and kingdoms. Ironically, several US states retained an established religion, but efforts to continue this arrangement soon ended. The last holdout was Massachusetts. Yet over the years, courts have had to decide what actions and symbols would constitute an "establishment" of religion. For example, does a monument listing the Ten Commandments that's placed in front of a government building constitute establishment?

On the one hand, state governments have set forth their own laws that have led to the removal of Christian, Jewish, and other religious symbols from state, county, and city buildings or parks. Mandatory prayer in school has been eliminated or curtailed, along with the performance of religious music in public schools.

On the other hand, government at all levels has continued to respect and support the exercise of religious beliefs in a variety of other ways. For example, the military provides chaplains of various religious faiths to serve its soldiers. And religious institutions of varying kinds are granted tax-exempt status for their property holdings and nonprofit functions.

The federal government and the states have sought to honor the "freedom clause" and to protect the free expression of religious beliefs. The Religious Freedom Restoration Act of 1993 was the most recent effort to provide protection for religious beliefs and activities in an increasingly secularized society. Freedom of religion is also supported by other provisions in the First Amendment, including freedom of speech, freedom of the press, and the right to assemble peaceably. Here again, courts will continue to decide how far the "freedom clause" can reach. For example, recent cases have addressed the question, Can a store owner or vendor deny services to someone based on his or her religious beliefs?

Though the promise of religious freedom has been clear from the beginning, the country has had an ongoing struggle to realize it. There has been a tendency for many to think of the United States as a "Christian nation." These voices expect privileges for Christians that are not available to others. The model reflected in this expectation is "Christendom"—a model born in medieval Europe. It is a social arrangement in which Christianity has a privileged status and the beliefs and practices of Christians are reflected in social attitudes, laws, and public policy. One relatively benign evidence of this outlook is that a Christian festival—Christmas—is a legal holiday.

Our nation's immigration policies have had a profound impact on our struggle with religious equality and our "Christendom" model. The Chinese Exclusion Act of 1882 was both racial and religious in its intent, with fears about the increase of Buddhist, Taoist, and Confucian expressions of faith on American soil. The rising number of immigrants from Eastern Europe, other Asian countries, and Africa brought similar fearful reactions as a result of changes in religious diversity.

One toxic outcome has been anti-Semitism. This was, of course, not an indigenous development. The seeds were carried across the Atlantic. They blossomed with the large influx of Jewish immigrants from Eastern Europe (starting in 1881) and reached full bloom in 1939. Though since then tempered in the population as a whole, anti-Semitism continues to surface, as it did in a particularly tragic way in Pittsburgh in 2018 and as it continues to emerge among advocates of white supremacy. The basic idea among white supremacists is that Jews do not belong here. Despite their small numbers (about 2 percent of the population), Jews are seen by these supremacists to be "seeking control" and in so doing are thought to be "undermining Christian influence." The roots of the fear of Jewish control can be traced back to a fraudulent "report" of an alleged meeting of Jewish leaders planning to take over the world. Called *The Protocols of the Elders of Zion*, it originated in Russia in 1903 and in 1920 was translated into German and circulated as factual by the Nazis. During the 1920s, Henry Ford printed an English translation and distributed five hundred thousand copies in the United States. The forgery continues to inform contemporary anti-Semitism.

A more recent toxic outcome has been a fear of Muslims. In some quarters, Islam is (mistakenly) portrayed as a violent religion, and Muslim immigrants are regarded as dangerous. They are thought to be undermining America from the inside. It is, of course, true that a small minority of Muslims, incorrectly invoking their religion, have adopted a militant, anti-Western outlook, but they do not reflect the mainline teachings of Islam. Distrust of Muslims and people of other non-Christian religions is another outcome of regarding the United States to be a form of Christendom.

The constitutional promise of freedom of religion was also often ignored in relation to the various tribes that we lump together as "Native Americans." The thinking in the nineteenth and early twentieth century was that they had to be "civilized" in order to be fully American. Native Americans suffered from the mistreatment of the US government in many ways, including the abandonment of treaties, forced relocation from their tribal lands, and mass executions of their people. Negative government policy also included pressure to abandon Native American religious traditions—a policy that was often enforced at the boarding schools the children were forced to attend. Not until 1978 was the American Indian Religious Freedom Act passed. Until then, many aspects of their religious practices and sacred ceremonies were illegal, despite the nation's public endorsement of religious freedom.

"Religious pluralism" is the outlook of the Constitution and Bill of Rights. No religion is to be given a privileged position. It is indicative of the ongoing confusion between "religious pluralism" and notions of "Christendom" that not until the 1940s did the Supreme Court formulate a clear distinction between "religion" and "Christianity." It did so as it dealt with a number of lawsuits regarding the Jehovah's Witnesses.

With the increase in the number of Muslims, Buddhists, Hindus, and other non-Judeo-Christian believers, America's promises of freedom of religion are again being tested. Some local communities, for example, have welcomed Muslims and the building of mosques. Other communities have exhibited strong opposition. Dialogue has increasingly occurred among Muslims, Christians, Jews, and others, often with strong denominational support. However, some Christian denominations have been silent or voiced fear and opposition. Political leaders have been of a mixed breed as well, from those who remind citizens of the American promises to welcome all people to those who play on the fear of change to gain votes.

AMERICA'S PROMISE AND THE ROLE OF THE CHURCH

Our nation has seen many times in its history when its people were divided by political, social, and religious beliefs, and times when people's beliefs and actions were driven by fear and uncertainty. At such times, we have often been blessed with national leaders who have shown courage and statesmanship and reminded us all of America's promises. President Franklin D. Roosevelt at the time of the Great Depression said, "Our Constitution was not a perfect instrument; it is not perfect yet. But it provided a firm base upon which all manner of men, of all races, and colors, and creeds, could build our solid system of democracy." He went on to articulate the "four freedoms" he felt were critical to our society: freedom of speech, freedom of worship, freedom from want, and freedom from fear.

We will always need political leaders who are moral leaders at all levels of our governing system. We welcome leaders who seek to unite us rather than divide us. As a democracy, we need to be open to a variety of opinions and engage in fruitful discussions as to how we can best move toward embracing our diversity, but our differences should not lead to a lack of civility or even hatred toward those with whom we disagree.

Throughout our history, we have sometimes received inspiration from national leaders, but more often, real and lasting change has resulted from the actions of local groups and individual citizens. As witnessed in the recent responses following the police-related deaths of George Floyd and other Black men and women, thousands of common folk have come forward to speak out and to call for the realization of America's promises. And the church has often played a prominent role in reminding us of these promises. The church has often led the way not only to get people at local and state levels to reach out to serve people of diverse backgrounds but also to call for our national leaders to take courageous action. The civil rights movement was born from the church and from the gospel challenges to love our neighbors and care for others, a movement that inspired both President Kennedy and President Johnson to work with Congress to change the laws of the land.

Clearly at this time, when our nation is again deeply divided and filled with the fear, anger, and uncertainty that comes with social and economic change, the church—in its various forms, including at the local level—must be more active than ever in bringing the message of God's love and our call to treat others with love and respect to a divided land. The fundamental purpose of this book is to demonstrate how we—as individuals and as members of our local congregations—can allow the moral guidance of the gospel and the promises of America to inspire us and direct us to serve the common good. In fact, we believe that Christians, in partnership with caring people from other faiths, should not merely remind Americans of these promises. We should, and can, hold them high, live out our Christian vocational call to action, and lead others to embrace and find great joy in our nation's racial and religious diversity.

CHAPTER FOUR

Challenges to Overcome and
Our Christian Response

Can America do it? Can it become the nation it is called to be by our founding constitutional documents? Can we hold our motto—"E pluribus unum" (out of many, one)—banner high and really mean it in reference to bringing not just states together to form one nation but America's people together? Can we Americans embrace religious and racial diversity not just in our laws but in our local communities, our schools, our places of work, our churches, our personal daily lives? Can we love our neighbors—without exception?

In order to respond to these questions with meaningful answers of "yes," we need to be honest about the challenges we all face. For Americans, moving beyond accepting the demographic facts of change to embracing both the current and the increasing religious and racial diversity in America will not be easy. In this chapter, we give specific attention to the challenges we face and, at the same time, begin to suggest how we as Christians have the capacity, the guidance of the gospel, and the call of our Christian vocation to meet these challenges.

MISUNDERSTANDING THE NATURE OF
RACE AND RACIAL DISCRIMINATION

In the widely-read children's novel *Maniac Magee*, written by Jerry Spinelli in 1990, the eleven-year-old orphan white kid Jeffrey Lionel "Maniac" Magee finds new life with a family in the segregated Black "East End" side of a Pennsylvania town. As the book describes, he loved "the people colors" he saw there, but "he couldn't figure out why these East Enders called themselves black." Instead, he describes the colors he found as "gingersnap and light fudge and dark fudge and acorn and butter rum and cinnamon and burnt orange." At the same time, the East End kids labeled Maniac as "white." Yet Maniac, after examining himself carefully, "came up with at least seven different shades and colors right on his own skin, not one of them being what he would call white (except for his eyeballs, which weren't any whiter than the eyeballs of the kids in the East End)."[1] In other words, Maniac learned that, instead of embracing our rich variety of skin colors in our American society, we tend to oversimplify and quickly place people into one racial group or another.

The Bible reinforces this idea that, no matter what color we call our skins, we are all created in the image of God (Gen 1:26–28). Rabbi Shai Held, writing in the *Christian Century*, notes how the Genesis creation story describes God as creating animals "of every kind." However, Rabbi Held points out that when God gets to the creation of human beings and specifically of Adam, "the careful reader (or listener) expects to hear that God created human beings 'of every kind' and yet the refrain is missing. The earth-shattering implication is that there are no kinds of human being." Rabbi Held goes on to say plainly and forcefully that "biblically speaking, racism and bigotry in all their forms are both an abomination and a heresy, indicative of a brazen denial of God as creator of all."[2]

Indeed, the Bible does not contain any reference to the concept of race as it is now encountered in our modern society. As is evident when references are made to Ethiopians (whether in the story of Solomon or in the story of the Ethiopian eunuch baptized by Philip in Acts 8), skin color was not noticed. Not until the 1400s did the concept of race as a "social construct" come into being. It was used to distinguish people in sub-Saharan Africa and the New World from Europeans. Gradually, it came to include the idea of European superiority. Europeans were "advanced" and "civilized" while others were not. With the advent of the transatlantic slave trade to the Caribbean in the early 1500s and to Virginia in 1619, such ideas were used to justify the slavery of people with black skin color. In the United States, a system of permanent racial bondage developed. There had been no such thing in biblical times, but to justify their actions, slave owners appealed to references to slavery in the Bible, refusing to recognize that slavery in the ancient world was not racial. It was economic servitude or the result of military conquest and not related to skin color. Race is not a biblical concept; it is a much later social invention.

In America today, racial and ethnic categories are with us constantly. William Frey points out that racial categories "are neither completely biologically nor scientifically determined," yet Americans have consistently constructed such categories "in ways that play into national politics and stereotypes."[3] We quickly identify people as "black, white, brown, or yellow" for a variety of personal, social, and political purposes. People are asked, as a part of the US Census, to self-report their race. Individuals on the loose after allegedly committing crimes are identified in the media as white, Black, Hispanic, Asian, or by some other category. "Black Lives Matter" became a rallying cry following the killings of Black people by police officers in several cities. Some people countered with the slogan "All Lives Matter" but, in doing so, failed to realize that the "Black Lives Matter" phrase referred not only to tragic police incidents but also to long-term systematic racial discrimination, overt and covert, that still needs to be changed so that indeed "all lives" do actually matter.

Some persons, in support of the view that surely they have no racist tendencies, like to say, "I am color-blind." This "color-blind" approach just does not work. It fails to appreciate the value of another's cultural and racial heritage, fails to recognize the struggles that others may still be encountering, fails to recognize how much everyone is influenced by social patterns, fails to focus on the societal changes still needed, and in a very important way, fails to truly embrace oneself and other persons in their own beautiful and individual diversity.

None of us want to think that we have tendencies to discriminate against people of other races or to be biased in our thinking and perceiving, yet we humans often exhibit these tendencies. How does this bias happen in our lives? Dr. Jennifer Eberhardt, professor of psychology at Stanford University, has conducted a wide variety of scientific experiments with people to discover the roots of what she terms "implicit bias." She defines this form of bias in her groundbreaking book *Biased: Uncovering the Hidden Prejudice That Shapes What We See, Think, and Do* as follows: "Implicit bias is a kind of distorting lens that's a product of both the architecture of our brain and the disparities of our society."[4] She notes that for our brain to function more easily, we like to automatically place people into categories. Thus "simply seeing a black person can automatically bring to mind a host of associations that we have picked up from our society: this person is a good athlete, this person doesn't do well in school, this person is poor, this person dances well, this person lives in a black neighborhood, this person should be feared. The process of making these connections is called bias."[5]

Bias, discrimination, and racism have a negative effect on all of our society, but their impact is especially profound on people of color themselves, often in ways we do not realize. Dr. David R. Williams, professor of public health at Harvard University, has spent much of his research career documenting the profound negative physical and mental health results on Blacks that arise from discrimination and segregation. In a noted TED talk in 2016, he observed that every seven minutes in the United States, a Black person dies prematurely. Is this because Blacks are poorer and less educated? No. His research indicates that at every level of education, whites live longer than Blacks. He has been able, through detailed research, to discover that a major factor in this outcome is racism itself, including overt racism (like being stopped more frequently by police), implicit racism (like being treated with less courtesy), and poorer health services due to living in segregated communities. Dr. William's research was confirmed in deadly and drastic ways by the Covid-19 pandemic. Tracking reports of the virus indicated that Black deaths from Covid-19 were nearly two times greater than would be expected based on their share of the population. And in some states, such as Michigan, the rate of deaths was three or more times higher. For Hispanics/Latinos in forty-two states and the District of Columbia, their confirmed cases of the virus were a higher share than in the overall population. In eight states, the rate was more than four times greater.[6]

Many Americans are very uncomfortable with discussing racial issues. They believe that they do not contribute to the problems of racial distrust or racial inequality because as individuals they do not utter hateful words or deliberately undertake actions that might be harmful to people of other racial, ethnic, and economic backgrounds. However, the lack of open discussion with people of color often prevents whites from understanding the difficulties that arise from more subtle signals or remarks. Americans also fail to give attention to the structural issues and policies that prevent progress toward equality and justice. Rev. William J. Barber II, leader of the Moral Mondays movement and the current Poor People's Campaign, reinforced this point when he emphasized that "racism ultimately is about systems and structures."[7]

Our nation's focus on placing people into racial categories can often be helpful in tackling both personal and structural problems that produce discrimination. But it can also create a false picture of our country's emerging society. Demographers are beginning to take notice. The US Census Bureau now allows people of mixed race to choose one race or more than one race on census forms. According to the Pew Research Center, about 7 percent of Americans are mixed race, but that figure is growing rapidly. Pew notes that more than one-fourth of Asians and Hispanics marry outside their race each year. Sabrina Tavernise, in a *New York Times* article, asks, Are the children of these particular mixed marriages white? Are they minorities? Are they both? Currently, the Census Bureau assigns a nonwhite label to most Americans of mixed-white and other races. Tavernise reports that Richard Albas, a sociologist at the City University of New York, calls this "an outdated classification system."[8] If we are to embrace diversity, we need to allow people to be proud of their racial backgrounds, including the complexity of such backgrounds.

My (Bill's) oldest granddaughter, a recent high school graduate, is a beautiful child of a mixed racial marriage. I wonder: Will she be able to choose her own identity, or will she be quickly labeled by others for their own social or political purposes? Will she have the freedom to claim what she wants? Will she be judged, as Martin Luther King Jr. had envisioned, by the "content of her character and not the color of her skin"?

No matter how persons are counted or labeled, our country is moving toward greater racial diversity. We cannot depend on some of our social and political leaders, who often misuse the concept of race for personal or political gain, to lead the way toward embracing this diversity. Real change depends primarily on us—on people in local communities, local churches, and local schools.

We believe strongly that Christians can lead the way by encouraging dialogue, reaching out across racial lines both as individuals and as groups. And we believe that real joy can be found in joining with people of various colors in service projects for the common good. Christians can also play leading roles to bring about the structural and economic changes needed to make equal opportunity possible for all Americans. Indeed, gospel-led Christians are already entering into activities that will produce meaningful change and joyful rewards for all of us.

FAILURE TO RECOGNIZE THAT "I AM THE PROBLEM"

Let's bring our concerns about where changes need to occur closer to home. Let's admit that perhaps the most difficult challenge to overcome lies within each of us personally. As Dr. Eberhardt emphasizes, each of us (of all colors and backgrounds) lives daily with biases and stereotypes that can interfere severely with the goal of embracing both racial and religious diversity. Many of us are often uncomfortable encountering people of different races, or religions, or both. Worse yet, we fail to seek to understand why we feel uncomfortable. Placed in individual, personal language, many of us fail to admit that "I am the problem."

In 2009, a significant event in interreligious understanding and congregational decision-making occurred in Cordova, a small suburb of Memphis, Tennessee. In that year, the Memphis Islamic Cultural Center proposed to build a mosque on vacant land in the Cordova community. The parcel of land lay directly across the road from Heartsong Church, an active evangelical congregation. The congregation was immediately divided on whether to support or strongly oppose the plan.

Rev. Steve Stone, the pastor of Heartsong, gave strong leadership to encourage the congregation to welcome the Muslims to the neighborhood. Individual members were torn between following the pastor's lead or removing themselves from the parish. One member, struggling with his negative feelings about the proposed erection of the mosque so visible and near, came to Pastor Stone and asked for counsel. Pastor Stone listened carefully and encouraged the member to read carefully the words and actions of Jesus in the Gospels. He did so and was struck by the call of Jesus to love your neighbor and to welcome the stranger. He examined his beliefs, fears, and feelings, and tearfully concluded that "the Muslims are not the problem. I am the problem." He shared his new feelings with fellow members of the parish. Eventually, the Heartsong members put up a giant sign along the road by the church that read, "We welcome our new Muslim neighbors." They went on to invite the mosque members to use space in the church for worship while the new mosque was being built. Today the two groups hold many joyful events together. When individuals can recognize bias and seek to overcome their fear and discomfort, good things can happen![9]

"I am the problem" also occurs when we uncover our conscious biases but fail to recognize our unconscious or, in Eberhardt's language, our "implicit" biases. Influenced by media images, lack of information, and little interaction with others, we too quickly attach false and unhelpful attributes to various groups. We still see Muslims as potentially anti-American. We connect noted Jews with Hollywood or believe that all Jews favor Israeli policies in relation to the Palestinian people. These subtle biases often prevent us from forming friendships or at least from entering into useful dialogue with people of other races and religions. As a result, we continue to live with biases, stereotypes, discomfort, and fear.

Finally, "I am the problem" occurs when we witness other people exhibiting bias and we choose to remain silent. When we hear words of racial or religious bigotry being spoken, observe acts of discrimination, or are aware of racist institutional or public policies and we remain silent, we are in reality endorsing that behavior. Silence is a form of "action" on our part.

How do we move beyond our own biases, discomfort, and fear of the other? The Scriptures once again give us guidance. The apostle Paul points to the need to continue to think about our own potential shortcomings, even when we see ourselves as really "good people." He asks in Romans 2 that "if you are sure that you are a guide to the blind, a light to those who are in darkness, a corrector of the foolish, a teacher of children, having in the law the embodiment of knowledge and truth, you, then, that teach others, will you not teach yourself?" (Rom 2:19–21a). Teaching ourselves is a vital first step to seek to move beyond "I am the problem."

Moving from uncertainty and fear to embracing diversity is not always easy, but the Bible reminds us constantly not to be afraid, not to fear, and not to worry (see Matt 10:31; 28:10), and John reminds us that "perfect love casts out fear" (1 John 4:18). As we examine our overt and our more subtle biases, we should remember the promise of Jesus to always be with us. We can then move forward with confidence that engaging with others who are different from us will begin to replace discomfort and fear with new awareness, knowledge, acceptance, adventure, and even joyful celebration.

THE SPECIAL CHALLENGES FOR WHITE CHRISTIANS

Most of us who belong to churches have the experience of easy conversations. We talk over coffee after a Sunday morning service, we gather for church dinners, and we participate in various kinds of discussion groups. These are usually conversations among people who share a lot—a common faith, a similar socioeconomic background, a similar level of education, the same or an adjoining neighborhood. This experience may create the impression that reaching out and engaging with people across racial lines is equally easy. Most of us are likely not well prepared for the difficulty of what we are called to do. White Christians face at least three interlocking challenges.

Perhaps the least challenging of the three, but still vitally important, is getting to know people of color. White Christians need to listen openly and carefully in order to begin to understand the outlook and experiences of those on the other side of today's racial divide. What makes this difficult is taking seriously the reports of someone whose experience is so different from one's own. It is like being asked to see something one has never seen before. An important part of the challenge is resisting the impulse to dismiss or explain away what the other person is saying. Another difficulty is that the experience of people of color is in some ways the same and in other ways not uniform. Gathering a clear picture of racism requires listening for patterns.

White Christians have a tendency to view themselves as helpers, as persons with answers. In many cases, this tendency may be an asset. When reaching across racial boundaries, however, they need to resist this urge, because the goal here is fostering understanding and empathy, not providing advice or "doing something for" someone. What grows out of understanding and empathy is valuing the proposals of people of color and working *together* to reduce the debilitating effects of racism. More often than not, this requires effecting changes in the white world as much as it may involve changes for people of color.

Recognizing how much this teaching/learning expects from people of color is also of critical importance. It takes a good deal of trust to be candid when those whom society relegates to a lower social standing are explaining their experience to someone assigned a higher status. Many people of color have learned that it is prudent to defer to whites. A high level of trust needs to be built before anyone will risk candor, and this is doubly true when dealing with well-established patterns of isolation and misunderstanding. In these settings, when people of color share their experiences of what it is like to live in a racist society, it is an act of generosity and courage.

The second challenge for white Christians is to see themselves differently. Members of the dominant group tend to regard their experience as typical. They do not consider how distinctive it is. They do not "see" the privileges (or absence of hassles) society has granted them. Moreover, as members of the dominant social group, they tend to assume that the social values they have internalized are normative for society as a whole. They expect others to conform to those norms. It is hard to "see" what society has taught all of us to assume and to endorse.

When Darrell lived in Allentown, Pennsylvania, there was an older, quite outspoken woman on the city council. She complained frequently about Hispanics who kept furniture (old and new) on their porches in order to gather there regularly. She was assuming a priority of her own view of "neatness and good appearance." Not only was she generous with her criticisms, but she proposed city ordinances intended to make "them" comply. She failed to acknowledge that the Hispanic residents were doing something constructive: welcoming neighbors and building community ties. It is hard for members of the dominant group to "see" their priorities and how they affect their judgments.

Those of us who are "white" have grown up in a society that values whiteness and devalues dark skin. Those of us who are "white" have benefited—at least indirectly—from the cheap labor of the colored poor and have been in control of the institutions that run our economy and our society—manufacturing, retail, transportation, education, politics, and the like.

Drew Hart, a Black theologian who teaches at Messiah University, challenges us in a loving yet forceful way when he says to us that "white Christians especially need to learn about the development of race and white identity in America. Understand how it works so you aren't its puppet. Don't be afraid to talk about racism in spaces that will challenge and transform how you think." And then he continues, "Most of all, as people surrendered to the Holy Spirit, we must all ask God to reveal those areas in our lives that need God's transformative work."[10]

So the challenge for whites is to "step outside ourselves" and to look back and see ourselves as others see us. This is difficult. But it is also important, because progress toward racial equality requires that the dominant group understands its own role and its own self-interest in maintaining white privilege. Without this admission, significant change in the more subtle patterns of racism will not occur.

If white Christians fail to see themselves clearly, then white Christians will unfortunately join in the "status anxiety" of many other white Americans who feel threatened by the changes that are needed. Such a result will only make the inequities worse. The barriers will grow higher, and they will be more strictly enforced.

The third challenge for white Christians is to revisit the Scriptures, to see how God hears the groaning of a people enslaved and calls Moses not only to lead them out of slavery but also to go through a long training program where they learn to be *a* people rather than simply recreating the social hierarchy they had experienced. In their revisit to the Scriptures, white Christians will also see how Amos and other prophets side with the poor rather than the dominant group in Israel and hold out a vision for justice, mercy, and equity. And they will see how Jesus consistently identifies with the "unseen" people of the day. He stands with and stands up for them against the religious, political, and economic leaders who want them to "know their place." And then they will see how he was regarded by the authorities of his day—treated as a threat to the order of things that they considered to be essential. They will catch a glimpse of the "upside down" world Jesus envisioned.

The societal problem of Jesus's day was not racism, but it was a two-tiered society with effects very similar to racism. Those who sided with the Romans (including the high priest, the tax collectors, and many others) had the power, while the fishermen and shepherds and lepers and widows (the people with whom Jesus associated) were without influence. When Jesus calls Herod a "fox," when he heals the sick and feeds those who come out to hear him teach, when Jesus formulates the Beatitudes, he is wrestling with widespread societal problems, not just the personal problems of his listeners.

To return to Drew Hart, addressing the church, "When considering the racial problems in the United States, we must begin taking the New Testament Jesus more seriously, in all of his subversive and troubling implications for our social order."[11] Hart explains, "Jesus has started a kingdom rebellion in which his citizens love their enemies, redistribute their resources justly, forgive one another, treat the poor with dignity, live in solidarity with the vulnerable, and liberate the oppressed, all because they worship and praise the God of Jubilee who has been revealed."[12]

To be sure, this third challenge extends beyond those in the dominant culture because the pervasive racism of our society also affects people of color and often prompts them to see themselves as less worthy. The Christian message that we are all created by God and continually loved by God means that people of color are to be valued by themselves as well as by "whites." All are called to work for justice and for a society that respects the dignity of all.

For Christians, what the combination of seeing others differently, seeing themselves differently, and seeing the Scriptures differently yields is a divine invitation to turn around (the root meaning of "repent"), to turn away from the social pattern of racism (which does not square with God's intent), and to leave behind those attitudes and practices that contribute to it—and then turn toward the biblical vision of a whole, healthy society. This shift is the most important challenge. It is our calling.

Christians need to lead the way because they have experienced the grace of God and can count on that grace to accompany them through the "turning." That grace assures white Christians and Christians of color alike that our status is not determined by the norms of society but by the decisions of God. The freedom to change is grounded in the security of God's generosity.

A variety of experiments have been done to determine the most effective way to introduce change into a community. In every case, the result has been the example of neighbors. As people change and influence their neighbors, the assumptions of society will also be affected. Christians (along with others who care) are called to lead the way past racism to something more just and more humane. In the neighborhoods where they live—and beyond—their responses and their examples will matter.

THE NEED FOR STRUCTURAL AND POLICY CHANGES

In seeking to overcome the challenges that will allow Americans to embrace racial and religious diversity, we consistently point to the gospel message to love others—without exception. This challenging message calls for a change of "mind" and "heart" in order for individual persons to overcome biases and to open themselves to others. But to make this message meaningful and lasting, all of us must go much further. We must also examine the structural, systemic, economic, and policy changes that need to take place in our society to fulfill America's promises of racial equality and religious freedom.

What is it like, for persons of color, to live daily in a culture of structural racism? An African American friend of Bill's, Richard Green, holds a PhD in chemistry; has served as a professor, academic dean, and president at several higher education institutions; and is a fellow member of The Registry, the nation's largest placement agency for higher educational interim leadership. He and his wife have retired near Tucson, Arizona. He recently wrote these words for a Registry newsletter in response to the new focus on "Black Lives Matter" after George Floyd's death: "On many occasions I have experienced questionable approaches by local police in different communities. I understand too well the high anxieties when black males are stopped and approached by police. During the past six months,

I have been pulled over several times by Tucson police for no reason other than driving my car in the streets of the city. Fortunately, each time, after questioning, I was not given a citation and was asked to move on."[13] If this encroachment into a person's life can occur to a university president who happens to be Black, think of the daily harassment and prejudice experienced by so many people of color on highways, streets, and stores and while seeking employment or a new home to buy or rent.

Racial inequality and racism are embedded in America's social, political, and economic structures. When Rev. William Barber states that "racism ultimately is about systems and structures," he is not the only religious or academic leader emphasizing the need for systemic change. Ibram X. Kendi, professor of history and founding director of the Antiracist Research and Policy Center at American University in Washington, DC, describes how long-term policies, structures, and practices in our country continue to foster negative race-related results as well as negative opinions and perceptions. Kendi gives prominence to the role of "policy" in racism, in preference to such terms as *institutional racism* or *structural racism*, because "policy" points more directly to where the problems lie and how they can be addressed: "By policy, I mean written and unwritten laws, rules, procedures, processes, regulations, and guidelines that govern people."[14]

Who then is a racist? In Kendi's view, a racist is "someone who is supporting a racist policy by their actions or inactions or expressing a racist idea." On the other hand, an antiracist is "someone who is supporting an antiracist policy by their actions or expressing an antiracist idea."[15] For him, there is no neutrality. At any given moment, a person is either a racist or an antiracist, either following racist policies or opposing them.

Racist policies and individual bias are interrelated. A powerful example is found in our criminal justice system. When Americans see so many Blacks being stopped by police, so many Blacks who are stuck in jail awaiting a future trial, and so many people of color at disproportional levels in our state and federal prisons, many have an image in their minds that Blacks and others are simply more crime-prone. This conclusion then spreads to other biases in our daily lives in towns, schools, and places of employment. As Dr. Jennifer Eberhardt of Stanford University has articulated so well, "Addressing bias is not just a personal choice; it is a social agenda, a moral stance."[16]

So why are so many people of color caught up in our justice system? The answer is complex. According to Michelle Alexander, the author of *The New Jim Crow: Mass Incarceration in the Age of Colorblindness*,[17] part of the answer is the War on Drugs because it has rewarded police departments for the number of arrests and convictions, and it is easier to make arrests and get convictions in a poor neighborhood than in a middle-class one, where residents have more access to lawyers and people with influence. Thus even though many studies have shown that the use of drugs is as high or higher in white neighborhoods, many more people of color who are also poor are arrested, convicted, and sent to prison. Alexander says, "Federal funding flows to those state and local law enforcement agencies that dramatically boost the sheer volume of drug arrests: it's a numbers game. Agencies don't get rewarded for bringing down drug bosses or arresting violent offenders. They're rewarded in cash for arresting people en masse. Ghetto communities are swept for their low-hanging fruit—which generally means young people hanging out [on] the street corner, walking to school or the subway, or driving around with friends. They're stopped and searched for any reason or no reason at all."[18]

The same is true of traffic stops. Two studies of traffic stops in New Jersey and Maryland in the 1990s showed that "15 percent of all drivers on the New Jersey Turnpike were racial minorities, yet 42 percent of all stops and 73 percent of all arrests were of black motorists—despite the fact that blacks and whites violated traffic laws at almost exactly the same rate."[19] Along a stretch of I-95 in Maryland, African Americans comprised only 17 percent of drivers, but they were 70 percent of those who were stopped and searched, and "what most surprised many analysts was that, in both studies, whites were actually *more likely* than people of color to be carrying illegal drugs or contraband in their vehicles."[20] The problem of structural racism is that the white drivers had no clue that they were being treated differently. Their experience did not match the experience of people of color.

Dr. Eberhardt of Stanford points out the ongoing negative effects on families from these practices in our criminal justice system and the resulting mass incarceration. She notes that, according to a national survey of children's health, approximately five million children in the United States have a parent currently or previously in prison. Many of these children suffer from poor self-image, from mental and physical problems, and from a lack of parental and societal support. She notes that they "are significantly more likely than other children to wind up behind bars themselves."[21]

That conclusion is reinforced by the important work and service of the US Dream Academy, founded by Seventh Day Adventist pastor, national church leader, and magnificent gospel singer Wintley Phipps. It focuses on reaching out to sons and daughters of prisoners at early ages in their lives. Through after-school programs in a variety of large American cities, the academy provides mentoring and educational support to help these young children see that they can have a different future. More programs like this one are clearly needed to break through the cycles created by our ongoing racist structures and to prevent built-in biases we too quickly inherit.*

In other words, in addition to liberating hearts and minds, embracing racial diversity calls for us to work together to ensure that all people have

- access to stimulating preschool experiences for their children;
- excellent education in well-funded elementary and secondary schools;

---

* Bill served as chair of the board of the US Dream Academy for twelve years. The organization has centers in eight major cities and has enjoyed strong support from Oprah Winfrey; Rev. Barry Black, Chaplain of the US Senate; and other national and local leaders.

- equal opportunities for college and vocational school education and training;
- meaningful work with adequate pay;
- access to affordable health care;
- fair treatment by law enforcement on city streets and in our justice and penal systems;
- affordable housing that allows for a significant increase in choice of neighborhood living environments; and
- equal opportunity to register and vote in local, state, and national elections.

The good news is that racism and racist policies do not have to continue to prevent America from realizing its promises. In these hopeful words, Dr. Kendi of American University states his strong belief in the possibility of a different future for our society: "Racist power is not godly. Racist policies are not indestructible. Racial inequalities are not inevitable. Racist ideas are not natural to the human mind."[22]

Indeed, attention to unjust patterns and policies, not just individual failures, is critical to improving race relations. The same is true concerning the mistreatment of those who practice religions other than Christianity. Governmental religion-related policies and practices, the adoption of state and local educational curricula, and the teaching and practices of some Christian denominations often impede an affirmation of religious diversity. We have earlier described immigration practices and policies that have discriminated against specific religions, especially Islam in recent years. Local governments have also acted against the building of mosques and the worship centers of other religions through zoning laws or other legislative rulings. Some states, in adopting required curricula for their public schools, have prevented students from learning about religions beyond references to the Christian or Judeo-Christian heritage. For example, several Southern states currently are seeking to require the teaching of the Christian Bible as an academic subject, with no opportunity to learn of the contributions of other religions to American life, history, and culture. Moreover, some Christian denominations, misunderstanding the nature of faith—as described in chapter 2 of this book—have discouraged any teachings about other religions or any dialogue with people of other faiths. These systemic roadblocks must be addressed if our nation is to obtain a true sense of religious freedom and build friendly and valuable relationships with brothers and sisters of other faiths.

Thus Christian denominations and individual congregations must not only inspire each of us to open our hearts and minds to love our neighbors of other colors and religious beliefs; they must also give leadership to addressing the structural and policy changes necessary to make life, living, and interracial and interfaith relationships better for us all. As a meaningful part of a call to Christian vocational service, we move from love and concern to advocacy. As individuals, as denominational leaders, as pastors, as members of congregational action committees, we are called to advocate for the critical changes in structure, laws, policies, and practices that give even greater meaning to the words *love your neighbor—without exception.*

LACK OF A SENSIBLE AND MEANINGFUL IMMIGRATION POLICY

One critical area of public policy that affects both interracial and interreligious relations is immigration. Despite our great heritage as a nation of immigrants, America continues to struggle with immigration. The current policy for admitting immigrants favors persons linked closely to families who are US citizens, persons sponsored by employers, individuals suffering from persecution in their home country, and persons who compete in an online lottery, with certain countries (like India and Mexico) eliminated from the lottery. Under Trump administration policies, the number of new immigrants allowed annually into America was radically reduced (from about 110,000 to 18,000, and then almost to zero) despite the fact that most economists recognize the very positive impact that immigrants have made and continue to make on improving our economy. Under the Biden administration, the number is increasing, with plans to restore the total to previous levels.

In reality, the US immigration situation is a mixture of reasonable legal requirements, outdated laws, uneven enforcement, and uncertainty about future direction. The situation is complex. There are millions of undocumented immigrants, there are young adults brought to this country as children (the Dreamers) uncertain of their futures, and there are employers in need of immigrants with a variety of scarce skills. "False news" about the number of immigrants and their backgrounds creates unfounded fear among current citizens about whether these immigrants will be "good" or "bad" for America. Some politicians then stoke such fears and seek votes from those who want to curtail immigration, especially from countries with people of color or non-Christian religions. The image many Americans have is that all undocumented immigrants come across our southern border. But approximately half arrive in quite another way and come from all parts of the world. They arrived legally on a visitor's visa, often to care for a spouse, a child, or an elderly parent who is a citizen. When their visa expires, they have to choose between leaving the United States and not being permitted to return for six to ten years or overstaying their visa. If they choose the latter, they are numbered among the undocumented immigrants.

There clearly is a need for a new, more meaningful, sensible, and helpful immigration policy. Yet political representatives on both sides of the aisle have lacked the will and courage to come together to forge a new comprehensive policy. In 2007, a bipartisan Senate reform bill that would address most of the problems outlined above received a large number of votes but ultimately failed to pass. The bill provided a careful road map to citizenship for undocumented workers, gave support to the Dreamers, and addressed the critical needs of American employers for immigrant workers. Another bipartisan bill was introduced in 2013 but, to date, has gone nowhere.

The Trump administration sought to end the Deferred Action for Childhood Arrivals (DACA) program that had been initiated during the Obama years. The Supreme Court ruled that Trump and colleagues had not provided adequate reasons for discontinuing the program, but the justices left the outcome to be decided later. Impacted by the outcome are the lives of more than seven hundred thousand Dreamers. DACA is ultimately about the lives of our neighbors who have grown up and been educated in America and are vital, important members of our local communities.

Again, it will take lots of people at the local level, district by district, state by state, to urge Congress to give serious attention to a new, comprehensive, and more equitable approach to immigration. Doing so would allow many more Americans to move from fear, misinformation, and mistrust to embracing increasing racial and religious diversity.

Christians can and should take the lead in helping to foster a broad, sensitive, humane approach to immigration. The Bible provides lots of help and inspiration for doing so. In the Old Testament, the Lord says to Moses, "The alien who resides with you shall be to you as the citizen among you; you shall love the alien as yourself" (Lev 19:34). Then in the fortieth year in the wilderness, Moses gives instructions to all the Israelites to "love the stranger, because you were strangers in the land of Egypt" (Deut 10:19). The psalmist reminds us that "the Lord watches over the strangers" (Ps 146:9). The prophet Zechariah calls on all of us to "not oppress the widow, the orphan, the alien, or the poor" (Zech 7:10).

In the New Testament, the words of Jesus are clear and powerful. We welcome Jesus into our homes and hearts when we welcome the stranger (Matt 25:35, for example).

For decades, both Christian and Jewish groups have been at the forefront of helping immigrants and refugees settle in American communities. Groups such as the Community Refugee and Immigration Services of Church World Service; the Migration and Refugee Services of the US Conference of Catholic Bishops; HIAS (Hebrew Immigrant Aid Society), a Jewish refugee agency; and the Lutheran Immigration and Refugee Service have worked with local churches and synagogues to resettle people into new homes and communities.

However, with the actions of the federal government to decrease significantly the number of refugees and immigrants coming to America, our nation's resettlement system was slowly dismantled, impacting negatively the services that can be delivered. It is estimated that the country "lost one-third of its capacity to welcome and resettle refugees in local communities."[23] These agencies are now working hard to restore their capacity to assist refugees and immigrants once again.

Christians can respond to this changing situation by continuing to work in their churches to sponsor immigrant families, welcome the stranger, and help them adjust to American life and the local scene. But we must also mobilize at local, regional, and national levels of the church to advocate strongly and boldly for comprehensive immigration reform. We are called to do so!

ISOLATION AND THE TRIBAL MINDSET

While many communities in America are becoming more integrated in relation to both race and religion, a high percentage of Americans are still clustered in segregated neighborhoods and segregated circles of daily life. A 2013 survey by the Public Religion Research Institute discovered that "on average, the core social networks of white Americans are a remarkable 91 percent white and only one percent black. Moreover, three quarters of white Americans have completely white core social networks."[24] This situation means that most Americans do not have a full understanding of the challenges that Black people (and people of other races) often face. They also do not have the opportunity to interact with and develop close friendships across racial lines.

And the results of this isolation affect both white and Black individuals and families. In the late 1960s, I (Bill) served as a "community lay minister" at a Lutheran church in the Black community of Mantua in West Philadelphia. My young family and I lived on a narrow street in Mantua, and for three years, we were literally the only white folks in an area of approximately fifteen thousand Blacks. Fifty years later, the Black-white ratio in Mantua is about the same! Far too many Blacks and whites are still living out the results of long-term laws, practices, and economic conditions that tend to separate racial and ethnic groups.

We Christians also tend to separate ourselves into like-minded religious groups. We do so both within Christianity and in relation to people of other faiths. Despite our many ecumenical initiatives among denominational leaders, many Christians do not take time to reach beyond their "cultural church homes." As Rev. Jason Micheli, pastor of Annandale United Methodist Church in Virginia, has written, "People select churches on the convictions in which the culture has already formed them. This is why so many Christians know so few Christians who disagree with them. It's why our ecclesial culture so neatly replicates the polarization in our wider culture."[25] This tendency, of course, carries over to a lack of meaningful relationships with people of non-Christian faiths and people with no church connections.

The "age gap" or "cultural generation gap" also contributes to our demographic divisions. This gap is especially wide between the older white population and the growing younger minority population. Based on a 2015 American Community Survey, William Frey points out that "Baby Boomers and seniors are more than 70 percent white, with blacks representing the largest racial minority. In contrast, millennials and their children are more than 46 percent minority, with Hispanics constituting the largest share of their minority population."[26] Earlier in America's history, older and younger generations lived closer together, especially among the same core families. With greater mobility and the emergence of retirement villages, often encouraging older Americans to move to Sunbelt "seniors only" communities, active cross-generational relationships are more difficult to maintain.

Forming ourselves into separate groups is quite understandable. Humans like to spend time with people who are most like them. For our society, however, problems begin to occur when tight group associations result in "tribal thinking." We humans like to have our gut feelings affirmed by others around us. We develop what the social psychologist Jonathan Haidt has termed "the righteous mind." Surely our views are correct because all the people around us affirm that we are correct. Haidt describes how Dale Carnegie was able to "win friends and influence people" by being a good listener of other people's views and seeking to understand other perspectives as a part of useful dialogue. Instead, many Americans fail at this wise practice because "in moral and political arguments . . . our righteous minds so readily shift into combat mode."[27] The other dangerous outcome of this tribal mentality is categorizing people who hold opposite views as "the enemy," the "rival team," or "bad people."

Can we Americans overcome this tribal thinking and move out of our isolated worlds? Yes, we can! And once again, the church has a critical role to play. As members of congregations, we are uniquely positioned to reach out to people of other faiths and backgrounds in our communities. We are also part of a much larger network of congregations and denominations that have the capacity to bring people together for productive discussions out of love and respect for one another. And the power of the gospel and the challenge of our Christian vocation can lead us away from tribal isolation toward open engagement with our neighbors.

THE CONTINUING REAPPEARANCE OF NATIONALISM AND EXPRESSIONS OF WHITE SUPREMACY

I (Bill) grew up in the small town of Hillsboro, Oregon, now a much larger suburb of Portland. In the center of town was a Grange hall, a community gathering place for area farmers and local community groups. When a Lutheran mission pastor came to Hillsboro in the late 1950s, a new congregation formed and began using the Grange hall for Sunday services. As members of this new congregation, my father, mother, and I fondly remember the inspirational worship services that took place in this special place.

In December 2018, the *Oregonian*[28] reported that this same Hillsboro Grange hall had recently been taken over by a white supremacist

"Sovereign America" group. Twenty-five civic-minded Hillsboro residents, including the mayor, attempted to broaden the Grange membership but were rejected. One of the Sovereign America leaders publicly declared that the recent election of a female Muslim to the US Congress was "repugnant to the United States of America's Constitution" and that she was "worthy of deportation, expatriation or imprisonment."

Most Americans reject the racist thinking of white supremacist and nationalist groups. They are aware that such groups, including the Ku Klux Klan and neo-Nazi groups, have existed at various times in America's history. But surely, they think, these groups are declining and have little impact on the general population. Not so! The Southern Poverty Law Center (SPLC)—the main tracking organization for extremist, militia, and hate groups in the United States—indicates that hate crimes and serious racial and religion-related incidents have increased since 2016. The center reported that anti-Muslim hate groups tripled in 2016.[29] (The 2020 report from the SPLC identifies 838 active hate groups throughout the United States.) The 2019 SPLC annual report also documented an alarming 55 percent increase of white nationalist groups since 2017. The report emphasized that white nationalism "poses a serious threat to national security and pluralistic democracy."[30]

Why this increase in such groups? Many individuals have their own special reasons for joining, including the influences of friends or parents, poor self-images, and the need and desire to be a part of a like-minded group. But the main focus of white nationalist messaging is the fear of white people becoming a minority. Such messages often incite fear by creating rumors of a conspiracy to weaken the "superior white race" through massive immigration and different rates of birth. They see anyone who questions such views as the enemy.

White nationalists label this demographic change as "white genocide." Recently, in a high school in southern Minnesota, someone spray-painted on the pavement at the school's entrance the words "Immigration is white genocide."[31] This conspiracy theory grows out of false perceptions and false teachings about a future of racial and religious diversity that should be embraced rather than feared. It fuels actions of self-doubt and hatred of neighbor, instead of love of neighbor.

Changing the mindset and the racist behavior of white nationalist groups is not an easy task. But individuals and church groups who believe in the value of all human beings and find meaning and joy in embracing racial and religious diversity can take important steps to change the atmosphere that creates such groups and gives them a hearing. We can start by teaching our children the gospel messages of love and respect for all God's people and remind ourselves and others that "love casts out fear." Parents need to become comfortable with talking openly about race and racism in our society. Cindy Wang Brandt, who writes frequently about faith and parenting, says, "Helping children develop a positive racial identity and providing them with antiracism tools begins with honest conversation."[32]

Those of us who care about human dignity can become part of peaceful demonstrations when church groups and others come together to send different messages to the American public—the messages of hospitality, kindness, welcoming, hope, and love found in the Old Testament, the Gospels, and the letters of Paul, John, and others. In 2018, white supremacist marches in Charlottesville, Virginia, resulted in the death of Heather Heyer, run down by a car driven by a neo-Nazi. In some of the photos of the event, one can see an interfaith group of clergy kneeling and praying. As they were taunted and spit on by the white supremacist group members, the interfaith group presented a courageous display of love against the marchers' display of hate. Later, signs were placed on the spot where Heather Heyer was killed that read, "One Human Race," "No More Hate," "Never Forget," and very critically for all of us, "The Minute We Stop Fighting Back, That's the Minute Bigotry Wins."[33]

FEAR OF CULTURAL CHANGE

Another challenge to overcome is a built-in fear among many people of having to change the cultural behaviors they have inherited. In

March 1965, I (Bill) was among a group of students from Union Theological Seminary and other higher educational institutions in New York City who answered the call to provide strategic assistance for Rev. Dr. Martin Luther King Jr. and the Southern Christian Leadership Conference (SCLC) in support of the now-famous Selma to Montgomery March. The march sought to rally support for expanding voting rights for African Americans who were kept from voting by long-standing, discriminatory Jim Crow laws throughout most of the Southern states. My assignment was to help with logistic support in Montgomery, Alabama, where the march would end. It was a dangerous time for the civil rights volunteers. They were trained by SCLC leaders to remain peaceful and to carefully avoid having whites and Blacks interacting too closely or even walking together. I remember vividly walking in Montgomery with several white volunteers, at least twenty yards behind several fellow African American volunteers, on the sidewalk in front of a large all-white mainline church on a Sunday morning. People emerging from their church service likely forgot the message of the gospel being preached that day. Instead, they stood with angry stares and made rude remarks directed at the volunteers from the North. Fear was on their faces as well. They recognized that their long-held culture of segregating races and of white power controlled by voting discrimination was being threatened.

Fortunately, much has changed in those Southern states among individuals, families, communities, and churches. Yet much still needs to change throughout America if our nation is to embrace a new culture of racial and religious diversity.

During the 1960s, I (Darrell) worked as an intern in a congregation in Washington, DC. Some of the members had come from other parts of the United States to work for the government. Others were native Washingtonians. While I was there, many of the latter group lived in areas where "block busting" was occurring. A Black family would move in, and realtors would try to scare others into selling at a low price. Ten years later, in the mid-1970s, I returned to work in the same congregation. When I visited with those who had resisted the block busting and stayed in their homes, they usually told me about the wonderful neighbors they had. The persons next door were "such nice people," and the couple across the street "would do anything to help." It soon became clear that all of these neighbors were people of color. But as the conversation continued, the stereotypes that I had heard ten years earlier would be repeated. The people they knew—their neighbors—were exceptions, but the stereotypes had not been abandoned. Personal relations are crucial, but changes in outlook are also needed—changes that are culturally and socially significant and of benefit to others. Unfortunately, these can be more difficult to bring about.

Significant change is hard. Psychologists have documented how change often produces significant stress in our lives. This is true even for positive changes such as moving to a new location, receiving an advancement in our employment, or even preparing for a special vacation. Psychologists call the results of these positive changes "eustress."

Stress is especially troublesome when it results from fear of the unknown. Sometimes fear can be helpful, as a person prepares to handle uncertain situations. Yet fear becomes irrational if people have been falsely informed. For example, people are sometimes made to fear immigrants because they "might commit crime," when statistics show that they have a much lower crime rate than Americans who have grown up here.

In a similar fashion, especially after the tragedies of 9/11, all kinds of anti-Islamic messages were circulated among the American populace, messages that claimed or implied that all Muslims, by virtue of their religious beliefs, were prone to engage in anti-American, anti-Christian, and anti-Western violent actions. These messages ignored the positive, peace-loving tenets of Islam and the patriotic support the vast majority of Muslims in this country give to America and the American way of governing.

As Carolyn Helsel, a Presbyterian minister, has articulated so well, "We are taught to fear. Noticing fear and talking ourselves out of that fear is essential if we are to overcome the biases we were often taught."[34] And as we have emphasized elsewhere, we are guided always by the reassuring biblical theme of "Fear not, for I am with you."

Yes, cultural change is difficult. But the American people have had a history of adapting to cultural change even though the ride was often rocky. We have embraced a broader religious culture—from Protestant to Protestant-Catholic to Protestant-Catholic-Jew,[35] or in shortened form, Judeo-Christian. A culture that fully embraces people of all colors is still being developed, but we have come a long way! And embracing a culture of racial and religious diversity can be led by congregations who replace angry stares with signs of love and hospitality, using the power of the true gospel message.

DEALING WITH MEDIA EXPANSION: POSITIVE AND NEGATIVE IMPACT

Developments in communication technology in recent decades have produced another significant challenge. Before the emergence of numerous cable channels, the internet, and social media, Americans got their news from three major TV networks, local and regional newspapers, and weekly news magazines. For the most part, Americans were hearing or reading similar news stories. We may have disagreed with our spouses, our aunts or uncles, or our neighbors about various issues, but we were essentially using common data and news reporting for our opinions and arguments. Americans live in a different media world today. This world of instant information sharing, on-site video recording, hidden cameras, and global media outreach can be helpful to us all—if the information presents a truthful picture, valuable ideas, and inspirational words that can help bring us together and not tear us apart.

Unfortunately, our media expansion has also produced significant divisive media, often slanted toward specific political, social, and religious viewpoints. All of us know relatives, neighbors, and fellow workers who tend to listen only to specific radio talk shows, watch a favorite news channel, or go to those internet sites that reinforce views they already hold as "truth." Eberhardt says that this tendency leads to what she labels "confirmation bias." This practice removes any different ideas from consideration and produces "a mechanism that allows inaccurate beliefs to spread and persist."[36]

As a result, we Americans have divided ourselves into opposing "teams" or "loyalty groups." And our selection of media sites that support our views concerning race, religion, politics, social customs, or the world in general tends to increase the divisions among us. As Justin Lee, who seeks to bring people across our cultural divide together for meaningful dialogue, has written, "Team loyalty is a massive hurdle for any cross-divide dialogue. In our polarized society, people tend to see the world in terms of opposing teams, defined by whatever they see as important—politics, religion, social circles, etc. They trust the information and opinions of people on their 'team,' and they mistrust the information and opinions of their opponents' teams."[37]

Social media that intended to bring people together, like Facebook, Twitter, Snapchat, and other sites, have instead often exacerbated the problem, for several reasons. First, some social media sites can quickly spread misinformation. Facebook, a major distributor of news for millions of people, has been severely criticized because, as Maria Ressa—CEO of an online Philippine news site but writing in *Time* magazine—has argued, Facebook "refuses to act as a true gatekeeper, allowing lies to spread faster than truth. For that, I'm among Facebook's worst critics."[38] In the summer of 2020, the Anti-Defamation League, joined by the NAACP and other civil rights groups, organized a "Hit Pause on Hate" advertising boycott campaign aimed at Facebook's failure to deal with messages of hate and ongoing harassment by various groups. Joining the boycott were major companies, including North Face, Patagonia, Unilever, Ben & Jerry's, and Verizon, causing Facebook's stock price to drop. Facebook finally responded by promising to hide or block content considered hateful and false claims related to political election campaigns. Second, social media users often communicate via soundbites and terse summaries of more complex situations, a practice that makes understanding and open dialogue more difficult.

The gospel calls us as Christians to pursue the truth, for "the truth will make you free" (John 8:32). And the eighth commandment calls on us to "not bear false witness against our neighbor." Fortunately, many Christian congregations are recognizing the impact of divisive media, and they are encouraging people to expand their minds and be open to listening to other viewpoints. The power of the gospel's call to pursue the truth, not live in fear, and love ourselves and others will continue to lead the way.

Congregations are also recognizing the power and potential of social media and new communications tools for very positive uses. Forced by the Covid-19 virus to use online means of worshipping and conducting business, congregations have utilized YouTube, Facebook Live, Zoom, and other electronic means in innovative and inspirational ways. Congregational committees and councils have continued to meet and make important decisions. Worship and preaching have reached people still hungry for linking with fellow parishioners. Not only large congregations with greater experience in using electronic communications but also smaller rural congregations have adapted to the challenge. Expanded communication technology can also be very helpful in the future for connecting with diverse racial and religious groups. Going forward, even when congregations return to more normal worship and meeting practices, they will have learned that the gospel messages of love and truth can reach people in a variety of ways.

POLARIZATION AND INCIVILITY

The disappearance of a sense of civility is another big challenge in our current polarized society. In the 1960s, both of us (Darrell and Bill) studied at Union Theological Seminary in New York City. Its faculty members were often very critical of the ethical values reflected in governmental, corporate, and even denominational policies and actions. Yet their criticisms were made with a sense of civility more than arrogance. I (Bill) remember distinctly a class in ethics, taught by Dr. John Bennet, who urged his students to make ethical decisions with a combination of boldness and caution. He said, in effect,

Be leaders in living out the gospel message; be prepared to make courageous decisions out of your ethical concerns; yet, always do so with a sense of trepidation, knowing you do not always have the final answer. Only God has that answer!

Today, in much of our polarized American society, a sense of civility is missing. Language in personal conversations, social media, and public demonstrations is often filled with name-calling, racial and religious stereotypes, and labels. Labels seem to come from all sides. Here's a sample of how other people have been labeled in recent years: liars, terrorists, junkies, deplorables, Jihadists, criminals, dumb, ignorant, bad. Labeling people quickly cuts off the possibilities for meaningful dialogue and mutual understanding. Increasingly, we Americans see certain other Americans as the "enemy," and we place a label on them to protect our ego and to downgrade their status.

Why have we reached this point in a country that many still see as the greatest experiment in democracy? James Hankins, a professor of history at Harvard University, has decried this trend toward incivility and points to poor expectations we set for both youth and adults. He states, "One reason that fewer people are civil today is that fewer people know how to be civil; fewer people even know what civility is, so fewer people value it."[39] Civility is, in Hankins's words, "the forgotten virtue."

When people lived together in rural, small towns or urban neighborhoods, they understood that they needed each other. For example, the local grocery store owner knew that he needed to get along with his neighbors because they were his only customers. They could not be replaced. New social arrangements no longer require learning and practicing the same communication skills because the relationships have been depersonalized.

Michael Ignatieff, noted historian and journalist, has traveled the globe to explore how multiethnic and multireligious communities have learned to live together. In two American inner-city neighborhoods—Jackson Heights, New York, and South Central, Los Angeles, California—he demonstrates how various groups have in effect adopted the "virtue of tolerance" in order to "generate collaboration among strangers who do not share a common origin, religion, or ethnicity."[40] Tolerance, akin to civility, becomes, in his mind, among the "ordinary virtues" along with trust, honesty, politeness, forbearance, and respect.

As Christians, we are called not only to exhibit civility or tolerance but to go even further—to love our neighbors as ourselves. Instead of creating enemies by labeling, negative name-calling, and other acts of incivility, Jesus challenges us to "love your enemies" (Matt 5:44). And the apostle Paul expands the "ordinary virtues" with his list of the "fruits of the spirit" to include "love, joy, peace, patience, kindness, generosity, faithfulness, gentleness, and self-control" (Gal 5:22–23). These are lessons in civility! Here again, Christian churches can use these profound messages to help rebuild a sense of civility in our society.

FALSE UNDERSTANDING OF THE
PROMISES OF OUR DEMOCRACY

America was born with the promise that all people were created equal. Yet as most of us are aware, that promise was limited throughout our history and has favored both Christians and white folks. With the significant increase in both racial and religious diversity, we now face a new challenge and a new opportunity.

For the American promise that "all are created equal" to be realized, significant changes in both individual attitudes and economic and social structures will need to occur. Together we will need to make sure that all voices can be heard in our democratic system. As Eboo Patel has written, "Our country may have had more 'coherence' of a kind in an earlier era, but a good deal of that coherence was only made possible by suppressing or excluding dissenting or unheard voices."[41]

More voices are being heard throughout our political and social systems. The membership of the US Congress has become more diverse with people of varying racial, national, and religious backgrounds.

Yet much of our current rhetoric points to divisions in our various "identities" rather than unity and the common good. "Identity politics" tends to divide people and issues by race, sex, ethnicity, national origin, and religious affiliations. Francis Fukuyama, noted political theorist, in a recent presentation at the University of Pennsylvania warned that democracy suffers if "everyone is aligning into identity groups that are fixed by the way you were born." Instead, he calls for "civic identity" based on universal American principles, including "belief in the U.S. Constitution, in the rule of law, in the principle of equality embodied in the Declaration of Independence. You would say an American is somebody who believes in these things."[42]

To realize this original view of "who is a true American," we will all need to change. "Identity politics" might be helpful to some in the short run, but both of our major political parties will need to change in strategy and outlook if they are to succeed in the long run. Appealing to specific racial or religious (or nonreligious) groups might sometimes bring short-term political victories. But identity groups will change in size and loyalty over time. In other words, both parties need the broader visions of great Americans, such as Abraham Lincoln and Martin Luther King Jr., who fought difficult battles in American society but called for the rights of all to be protected in order to achieve a sense of unity in the long run.

To realize the promises of our democracy, we must also continually give attention to the issue of voting rights. Those involved in the civil rights movement rejoiced in the passage of the Voting Rights Act of 1965 that outlawed many of the Jim Crow laws that prevented Blacks in Southern states from voting. Recently, the Supreme Court weakened the federal oversight of the protection of voting rights. A number of states and local communities have enacted new laws, policies, and practices that have made it more difficult for Blacks, other people of color, and immigrants to be able to exercise their right to vote. This is, once again, racism at work. These rights must be protected for the sake of our democracy and all its people.

Our nation's handling of the Covid-19 pandemic vividly brought forth another false understanding of the goals of our democracy. As

Americans, we rejoice in our freedom, and we have fought to protect this freedom. But for many Americans, the idea of "freedom" has focused primarily on "rugged individualism" to pursue the "American dream" without much regard for the well-being of others. Forgotten is the fundamental civic lesson, expressed by Eleanor Roosevelt in these words: "Freedom makes a huge requirement of every human being. With freedom comes responsibility."[43] Unfortunately, during our nation's battle with the Covid-19 virus, the wearing of masks to protect personal health and the health of our neighbors became for many an issue of "freedom." Some even claimed that the US Constitution gave them freedom—the right not to wear a mask, if they didn't want to. Forgotten was the fact that the mask was not primarily to protect oneself but to help prevent the spread of the virus to others. Forgotten was the responsibility to care about and help protect others in the community.

The Christian approach to the meaning of freedom provides even greater guidance and understanding about the call to serve others in similar situations. Through God's grace, we have been forgiven and freed from the burden of sin sitting on our shoulders. Instead, God grants us his righteousness. Martin Luther called this the "happy exchange." We are now freed to serve others. In the face of crises like the rapid spread of a virus, we use our freedom to care for and focus on the needs of the wider community. In doing so, we love our neighbors—and ourselves.

What do we as Christians have to offer to help improve our current political scene and to begin to make manifest the promises of America? Does the church have a role? We would argue yes, definitely. The call to Christian vocation not only creates worshipping faith communities but also takes us out of our urban cathedrals, our suburban sanctuaries, and our small rural churches into the world. We are led by the gospel of love to pray for and work for the changes in our society that bring people together, not tear us apart. We do so not just to save our democracy but to benefit and uplift us all—the diverse people who are all "Americans" and the diverse people of the world.

PERCEPTION OF A WEAKENED CHURCH

Throughout this chapter, we have examined the challenges that we all face if we are to begin to embrace a racially and religiously diverse America. And in each case, we have indicated that the Christian church, in its various structures—ecumenical, denominational, and local—can play a major role in moving Americans from resisting this diversity to embracing it.

But wait! Can the church really play this role? Are not mainline Protestant, Catholic, and more recently, evangelical denominations declining in membership? Is it not true that younger people are moving away from the church as they claim to be "spiritual but not religious," signaling that they do not want to be involved in organized religious structures?

While statistics might indicate the decline of church membership in America, there are other signs that now may be the best time for Christians and Christian churches to give bold and impactful leadership to help Americans embrace racial and religious diversity. A 2014 Pew Research study indicates that amid reduced congregational membership, those Christians that remain or have recently joined the church are stronger in religious devotion. The study indicates that "while fewer Americans pray daily or attend church services weekly or more, those who are religiously affiliated are actually showing more devotion to their faith." And for practicing Christians, 68 percent say that "religion is very important," an increase over a study done seven years previously.[44] And in many congregations, young people are returning when they see the church in action, undertaking social justice causes they believe are important, including the battles against racism and religious bigotry.

Martin Kaste, a National Public Radio correspondent and a member of Phinney Ridge Lutheran Church in Seattle, Washington, recently declared his devotion to the mission and service of his congregation in a society that often seems so nonreligious when he shared his faith and his love of neighbor in these words: "It can be a bit of a jolt (or witness) when we cheerfully explain to acquaintances why we can't make that Sunday morning soccer game or that we try to contribute through our church to causes such as world hunger, sheltering the homeless, or receiving a refugee family. It's important to show that even though mainstream culture now dismisses Christianity, we—their friends and neighbors—are still part of the church."[45]

The church, through its denominations and thousands of local congregations, has a network that reaches into virtually every community throughout our landscape. As Robert P. Jones, CEO of the Public Religion Research Institute, has written concerning our need to bring whites and nonwhites together, "With few institutions poised to play this critical role, America's churches could be a place where a national, substantive conversation about race finally begins."[46]

The civil rights movement of the 1950s and 1960s would not have happened without strong leadership by church leaders. The church can again play this leadership role today. But it must do so at all levels.

Denominational leaders are coming forward to speak out, either individually or in concert, to oppose racism and actions taken against people of non-Christian religions. Real change, however, must come and can come at the grassroots, concrete-streets level of the Christian church—in the congregations spread throughout inner-city neighborhoods, along suburban boulevards, and beside country roads. Here is where the gospel-led action can take place. Here is where meaningful dialogue can be held. Here is where people of different races and religions can be brought together to embrace diversity, to realize the promises of America, and to live out God's call to love your neighbor without exception!

CHAPTER FIVE

The Use and Misuse of Religion

Religion—as practiced by Christians and by people of other faiths—can be a powerful force for good in our nation and around the world. But religion can also be misused and abused. Understanding how religion has been and continues to be distorted and used in false and damaging ways is important for us in relation to our goals for embracing diversity. This understanding helps us make sure that our own faith is well founded and contributes to the good of our neighbors.

THE UNFORTUNATE HISTORY OF MISUSE OF RELIGION

Misuses of religious faith have happened again and again throughout history. The ancient Hebrews had to face the competition with fertility cults and idol worship from the beginning. They lived under Egyptian, Greek, and Roman rulers who worshipped other gods or claimed to be God. Starting in 198 BCE, for example, the Greek Seleucid rulers tried to force the Jews living in Israel to abandon their religion and worship the Greek gods. When Antiochus IV Epiphanes, the Seleucid king, desecrated the temple by constructing in it a statue of Zeus, the Jews revolted and war broke out. The resulting victory for the Jews led to the rededication of the temple in 165 BCE. Later, in 70 CE, the temple was destroyed by the Romans during the siege of Jerusalem.

During the 1600s, the Thirty Years' War raged through Europe. A major cause was the religious dispute between Protestants and Catholics. In what is now Germany, several million people died. Earlier, several crusades sent European Christians on a religious mission to free the Holy Land from Muslim control. Some of these crusades attacked not only Muslims but also Eastern Orthodox Christians. Untold numbers died. In the Third Reich of the 1940s, five to six million Jews were killed, ostensibly for racial reasons, but the misuse of faith was prominent among the Nazis because the law that defined who were Jews did so on the basis of the religion of their grandparents.

Religions have been misused for centuries by people of various faiths and by nations as they have linked religious beliefs and religious practices directly to nationalism and government control. Freedom of religion is replaced by the dominance of one religion over all others. The idea is to protect the dominant religion, but the unintended effect is to distort and misuse it. In the middle of the 1900s, a Hindu-Muslim conflict produced two countries: Pakistan and India. Wars in Punjab killed hundreds of thousands. The conflict in this region has not ended. From time to time, it flares up again. Buddhists in Myanmar have recently expelled the Rohingya people, who are mostly Muslim with a smaller number of Hindus, for reasons that seem heavily influenced by religion as well as ethnic differences. Recently in India, with political power resting primarily with Hindu leaders, signs of Hindu nationalism have appeared, with discrimination against Muslims and members of other religions. Like the old battles between Catholics and Protestants, conflict within various religions has led to war, suffering, and death. For example, in recent decades, thousands of Muslims have died from the wars between Sunnis and Shiites. Indeed, all religions, at one time or another, have been misused to foster conflict and authorize violence.

Jesus, as demonstrated in the Gospels, was very critical of the religious leaders of his day, pointing to their abuse of religion for selfish gains and the maintenance of political and religious power. Then in the early years of Christianity, followers of Jesus were often persecuted and killed by Romans because of their refusal to worship the emperor and the Roman gods. Jesus had warned of coming persecution for his disciples in the Sermon on the Mount when he said, "Blessed are you when people revile you and persecute you and utter all kinds of evil against you falsely on my account" (Matt 5:11). And at the gathering for the Last Supper, he foretold that "an hour is coming when those who kill you will think that by doing so they are offering worship to God" (John 16:2). The tables were turned when in the fourth century CE, under Emperor Constantine, Christianity gained greater acceptance, and later in 380 CE, it became the official religion of the Roman Empire. This in turn led to a close relationship between the church and the Empire and to persecution, including violent persecution, against those who failed to accept Christianity. Even after Christianity came to the American continent, it was not tolerant of other religious expressions. In the American colonies, leaders often did not allow Christians of other denominations, much less those practicing another religion, to worship freely. Only Pennsylvania offered full religious freedom.

Thus Christians should not be too ready to blame another religion and assume that it is the source of conflict. Christians need to look first at their own tradition and consider carefully how their religious beliefs are being used today. The same is true for Jews, Muslims, Buddhists, Hindus, and others.

MISUSE OF FAITH BY EXTREMISTS

The misuse of faith, often with terrible consequences, occurs in extremist movements. The US Commission on Interreligious Freedom gives special attention to three groups around the world: the Islamic State of Iraq (ISIS), the Taliban of Afghanistan, and Al-Shabaab in Somalia. These three receive special attention because in each case, they seek to exercise "territorial control." They force people in the areas they control to live by their beliefs, rules, and regulations. They distort and misuse their brand of Islamic religion by deciding first on a set of objectives for social and political control, and then they select particular elements from their religious documents or interpretations that seem to lend religious support for their cause. The key concept here is "selective." Their selectivity effectively distorts the religion while at the same time tying it too closely to the specific goal of exerting political, social, and cultural control. So, for example, ISIS has a record of killing both Christians and those practicing a different form of Islam.

This extremist behavior on the part of ISIS is contrary to the historic teaching of Islam that Jews and Christians are also "people of the book" who are to be tolerated by Muslims. Sayyid Syeed, a leader in the Islamic Society of North America, has made the case that the future of Islam lies with Muslims who live in pluralistic societies such as the United States because the self-understanding that develops in these settings is consistent with the teachings of Muhammed himself.

Extremism unfortunately continues to arise in America as well, and the misuse of religion plays a powerful role. White supremacist groups in our country will select misinterpreted passages from the Bible to justify violent attacks on Jewish Americans. Anti-Islamist groups or individuals will cite false beliefs about Islam and Christianity to justify their hatred for and violent actions against Muslims. Ethnic prejudice and religious prejudice get intermixed by these domestic extremist groups.

What causes individuals to become extremists? Studies have pointed to a number of causes, including youth growing up in homes without parental love and support, experiences of domestic violence, lack of good mentors, loneliness in teenage years, and beyond. Lack of self-understanding and self-love adds to a poor self-image. Social media networks increasingly play a role as well, attracting individuals to a particular ideology that provides them with a sense of belonging and purpose, along with a new structure of authority. They then receive ongoing support from this new group, especially if they continue to advocate for an often religiously distorted and religiously infused ideology.[1]

While these are general trends leading to extremist and sometimes violent actions, every case may be different. The shootings in the synagogue in Poway, California, in April 2019 are a case in point. The young man who walked into the synagogue and opened fire grew up in a caring, religious family. There is debate as to whether he was influenced by a misinterpretation of biblical teachings about Jews that he learned in the conservative evangelical congregation he attended regularly.[2] At any rate, he connected his religious beliefs to the white nationalist ideology he learned from the internet. His parents were devastated with his anti-Semitic outcome, and their comments reveal that it is often difficult to know what thoughts are inside the minds of others, even those who are close to us: "Our son's actions were informed by people we do not know, and ideas we do not hold. Like our other five children, he was raised in a family, a faith, and a community that all rejected hate and taught that love must be the motive for everything we do. How our son was attracted to such darkness is a terrifying mystery to us, though we are confident that law enforcement will uncover many details of the path that he took to this evil and despicable act."[3]

Faith, if rightly taught and rightly practiced, can play a critical role in preventing extremism to develop for youth and adults in our society. Parents, school and college educators, Sunday school teachers, citizens of our communities—we are all called to condemn hateful actions and words as an affront to both our gospel teachings and the promises of American civil liberties and freedom. And we are called to create the kind of social environment in which young people feel that they belong.

MISUSE OF FAITH IN AMERICA: FROM CIVIL RELIGION TO CHRISTIAN NATIONALISM

America has had a history of groups of people and even church denominations misusing faith for political, social, and cultural purposes. Particular Bible passages were used out of context to justify slavery, segregation, and Jim Crow laws, while the gospel message of loving your neighbor was ignored. Some Christians have misused the call to evangelize and "tell the Good News" to mean that they can have no respect for the religious beliefs of others. In doing so, they misunderstand the nature of faith.

In recent decades in America, another dangerous misuse of faith has become even more prominent. Back in the 1960s—following the election and inauguration of John F. Kennedy as president—Robert Bellah, a highly respected sociologist of religion, wrote an essay in which he described "American Civil Religion."[4] Bellah was puzzled about his observation that every president from George Washington to JFK had mentioned God in his inaugural address. How did this square with their support for the separation of church and state? What he found in the speeches was a "civil religion." Its essence was the idea that God had bestowed on America special blessings, and in return, America had a special responsibility to be a moral example for the world. It included the idea of sacrifice for the nation. And it had its own religious sites (e.g., Arlington Cemetery) and its own rituals (e.g., speeches on July 4). Though it had never been anti-Christian (as had been the case in France after the French Revolution), American civil religion has also not been specifically Christian. It makes no reference to Jesus or the church or any distinctively Christian beliefs. It has been broad enough to serve as an umbrella for a variety of religious groups. In the essay, Bellah wondered aloud whether civil religion would be resilient enough to guide the nation's exercise of power during its then newly assumed role in the world. To most scholars, it seemed that he was onto something.

The Christian faith should not be confused with American civil religion. Doing so leaves no room for our faith to challenge its actions. In the years since Bellah's essay was written, surveys have shown that church members who are the most active in their churches are more likely to confuse their Christian faith and American civil religion. This confusion threatens the integrity of the Christian faith. To be sure, there are places where Christian ethics and civic responsibilities overlap, but the two are not the same. There are also places where

Christian ethics must call into question civic developments. For the individual Christian, a higher loyalty belongs to God's vision for the world than to American civil religion.

In addition to not confusing Christianity and American civil religion, we need to honor another dimension of their relationship—namely, that American civil religion is healthier if it is held in check by loyalty to the Christian faith. Among many people, especially in the last several years, American civil religion (without this check) has taken on the more radical form of "American nationalism" or what some would describe as "Christian nationalism." Nationalism "baptizes" America, and for its believers, becoming a superpatriot is a "religious duty." Only America matters; cooperation with other nations and the welfare of other peoples is unimportant. Nationalism erects barriers among God's people and tends to heighten conflict between our nation and others. The rise in nationalism is a disturbing development. Though Christianity and civil religion—each understood properly—can overlap, Christianity and nationalism do not. Christianity should function as a check on patriotism, keeping it open, respecting the dignity of other peoples, rather than narrowing a person's ethical concern to Americans only. In practice, nationalism has the unfortunate effect of going even farther, narrowing ethical concern to only some Americans—to "true Americans"—to those who have a certain skin color or a particular allegiance or those who think and behave a certain way.

The problem of Christian nationalism has been recognized by the National Council of Churches USA in a special April 2021 policy statement entitled "The Dangers of Christian Nationalism in the United States." Two compelling sentences of the statement read as follows: "Where the Great Commandment (Mt. 22:35–40 and parallels) enjoins us to love God with all our heart, soul, and mind, and our neighbors as ourselves, Christian nationalists choose to narrow who is considered an American, to love only certain neighbors, and to regard others as enemies to be defeated, deported, or destroyed. Where Christ affirmed that 'my Kingdom is not of this world' (Jn.

18:36), Christian nationalists have equated the Kingdom of God with their vision of 'America.'"[5]

This dangerous trend toward American or Christian nationalism began during the Cold War, when the enemy was "godless communism" and many Americans thought our country was on God's side. The trend continued in the 1980s when some denominational leaders, in seeking to create a "Moral Majority," began linking themselves very closely with conservative partisan politics. In this way, one form of Christianity (evangelicalism) was linked with one partisan political ideology. This alliance sought political and cultural dominance in order to reclaim America for Christianity.

The operative word here is "partisan," because there are other appropriate ways for religion to influence our political decisions. An essential component of these appropriate ways is that they must serve the common good and not some narrow political belief. Indeed, informed by our commitment to our Christian vocation, we are called to enter the "public square" with a goal of rectifying past injustices, seeking to help disadvantaged groups just as Jesus did in his deep concern for the poor. But if religion is used to endorse a proposal that benefits one group at the expense of another while not rectifying an injustice, it is being misused.

Our nation was built on the assumption that citizens would actively participate in the governance of their neighborhoods and the political entities beyond their neighborhoods. This participation is crucial for the functioning of a democracy. But from the beginning, there were limits on who could participate. Those excluded from the public square included women, those without property, and slaves. New immigrants were often not welcomed, but in time they were able to participate effectively. Throughout its history, our country has needed to extend the boundaries of full participation. A challenge for citizens today is to prevent us from backtracking. Current examples of backtracking include voter suppression, gerrymandering, and accusations of voter fraud. Reaching out to include others in the process of deciding what is good for the neighborhood and the larger community is a civic as well as a religious calling.

One important place where contemporary Christian ethics and civic responsibilities overlap is respect for people who practice other religions and respect for persons of different races. They overlap in their shared commitment to remove the social barriers that result in unequal treatment. To say that they overlap, however, is not to say that they are the same. The most basic message of Christianity is that, out of sheer generosity, God chooses to overcome the estrangement that separates us humans from God and be reconciled with us. God's choice is an act of "radical hospitality"—welcoming into fellowship persons who have no "standing" of their own before God. This message is conveyed in a variety of ways, going back at least to the call of Abraham, but it is conveyed most directly in the person of Jesus, the Christ, in whom God came to seek us out and be with us. The radical hospitality of God informs our vocation. It calls us to a "constructive, enlarging engagement with the other."[6] Our vocation, in turn, forms and shapes the way we practice our citizenship.

WARNING: DON'T GENERALIZE!

Another critical way to avoid the negative consequences of religious misuse and misunderstanding is to avoid generalizations or stereotypes. To assume that all Muslims are like ISIS is to create a stereotype that distorts Islam and interferes with any possible mutual respect or cooperation. Mustafa Akyol, a Turkish journalist and author of the book *The Islamic Jesus*, believes that radical groups like ISIS have created a terrible "Dark Ages" view of Islam.[7] Some Muslim leaders go even further in asking us to place radical, violent groups outside true Islamic beliefs. On Easter morning 2019, members of Christian congregations and other innocent people in Sri Lanka were killed by radical groups carrying Muslim labels. In response, the chairman of a mosque in Colombo, Sri Lanka, said these strong words about the Easter attackers: "This is not Islam. This is an animal. We don't have a word strong enough to curse them."[8]

American Christians have sometimes overgeneralized concerning other Christians in their own country. My (Darrell's) father usually avoided or discounted stereotypes. Typically, his judgments were generous, and he actively worked to interpret one group to another. But he allowed one bad experience to shape his view of Roman Catholicism. A priest in the neighborhood where he grew up, when called to give last rights to a neighbor, would not come unless paid to do so. Quite understandably, this offended him. The problem arose when he generalized from one experience and the behavior of one priest to form a negative view of Catholicism. (Of course, he was also influenced by the more general anti-Catholicism of that time.) This view persisted until later in his life when he started to meet and converse with more Roman Catholics and learn about reforms that were introduced after Vatican Council II. His views then changed.

We all must be careful not to generalize people according to how the media tends to classify various groups. Evangelical Christians, for example, especially following the 2016 elections, have been characterized almost universally as racist, backward, angry, and "deplorable." Angela Denker, in her book *Red State Christians*—while pointing to her concerns about the misuse of Christian Nationalism among the evangelicals—nevertheless describes how many of these fellow Christians have a wide variety of views concerning race, religion, and the proper use of government.[9] When we overgeneralize, we fail to leave room to identify and pursue areas for common ground, important dialogue, and progress.

Generalizations that portray a religion or race in negative ways are, of course, dangerous because they dehumanize the other and can be used by someone somewhere to mistreat members of that group. But generalizations that are neutral or positive can also interfere. Portraying Asians as high achievers, for example, might seem benign, but it can lead to resentment or insensitivity to their struggles.

The way to avoid these consequences is for the members of one religion to seek to understand the other religion. We have deliberately used the word *understand* in this context because it has two dimensions. One dimension is gaining the knowledge necessary to interpret the other religion accurately. The second dimension is getting to know persons who practice the other religion. Understanding on this person-to-person level is crucial because no religion is merely a set of beliefs or teachings; it is, as we have said, a way of life.

OUR SPECIAL ROLE IN OVERCOMING THE MISUSE OF FAITH

Christians are called to care for their neighbors. Jesus's dialogue with the lawyer to whom he tells the parable of the Good Samaritan shows that there is no limit on who is included as "neighbor." Persons of other religions and races are "neighbors." Persons in other parts of the nation or the world are "neighbors." Describing them as "neighbors" rather than "strangers" or "aliens" or "enemies" is vitally important. For Christians to avoid mistreating others (as important as that ethical directive is) is not enough. We are also called to reach out to neighbors, stand up for them, refute stereotypes, and foster understanding.

The Reformation idea of the priesthood of all believers was intended not to say that individuals should be priests for themselves but that members of the faith community should be intermediaries for others in the community. They should speak to them of God's grace and should intercede for them before God. So in regard to people of other races and religions, Christians are to help their fellow Christians overcome fear, abandon stereotypes, seek understanding, and treat others with love and generosity.

Though this calling applies to Christians everywhere, it is especially important for Christians living in the United States today because we need to show others that our nation's "grand experiment" in religious freedom works in order for us to be able to recommend with any integrity that others follow the same path. How can the United States lobby other nations and their governments to practice religious tolerance if it is not happening here?

THE POWER OF RELIGION FOR GOOD

Because of the misuse of religion, as we have described above, some philosophers and secular leaders over the years have argued that religions and religious beliefs should be abandoned and rejected altogether. In contemporary society, many young people have identified themselves as the "nones" because of a lack of good experiences (or no experience) with organized religion.

In light of not only historical misuse but also recent misuse of religion, should religious organizations, religious learning, and religious practices be abandoned? We would answer with a resounding "No!" When the nature of faith, as described earlier in this book, is fully understood, and when we remember the central role that faith has played in bringing self-understanding and love for others into our world, we must work not only to affirm the important role of religion but also to make it even more relevant for improving our lives and the lives of our neighbors.

Religion can be misused, but religion can also be a powerful force for good in individual lives and in our society. The popular Jewish writer Bruce Feiler has documented in his books the misuse of religion, especially by extremists. At the same time, he strongly believes that religion, not politics, is the solution to bringing people together. In his book *Where God Was Born: A Journey by Land to the Roots of Religion*, Feiler describes his travels throughout the Middle East and his conversations with people of various faiths that lead him to conclude that "the only force strong enough to take on religious extremism is religious moderation." He summarizes his thinking this way: "Religion can only be saved by religion."[10]

Can religion save itself and our society? Can the power of faith help us as individuals and as communities to overcome our divisions and embrace religious and racial diversity? Our answer is yes to both of these questions. Even more strongly, we believe that faith—as rightly practiced by individuals, groups, denominations, and across religious boundaries—is the most critical factor in bringing us all together for the common good.

THE POWER OF RELIGION FOR INDIVIDUAL AND COLLECTIVE GOOD

Religion provides an anchor, a starting point for self-affirmation, for finding purpose in life, for actively seeking to make a positive difference in the lives of others. Feiler, in the same book mentioned above, notes his strong belief that "religion is central to helping people develop an identity that is more mature, having to do with morals and ways of living."[11] His personal testimony, following his journeys and discussions with people of various faiths, affirms this belief: "At the end of my travels, I came to view my relationship with religion as I do my relationship with God. I can no longer be a passive recipient. I must be an active partner."[12]

People of faith, with a positive sense of self, can then unite with others to strive for peace, fellowship, and reconciliation. Religions have demonstrated that they can bring people together to achieve so much that they cannot achieve on their own. Robert Putnam and David Campbell, in their study of religion in America, concluded that religiously observant people are "better neighbors and better citizens."[13] In America, we are familiar with the good things that our Judeo-Christian heritage has brought to our land, and we are now beginning to learn that other religions have much to contribute as well to our common good.

THE IMPORTANT LESSONS OF OUR CHRISTIAN AND JEWISH FAITHS FOR AMERICA

Both the Hebrew Bible (the Christian Old Testament) and the New Testament make clear that a person of faith sees oneself as part of a larger story. The biblical witness begins with the affirmation that God created the world and saw that it was good. It begins with an acknowledgment that we are all "kin," all created in the image of God, all part of one family. And it begins with an affirmation of relationships and community: "It is not good that the man should be alone" (Gen 2:18).

Along the way, it becomes clear that God's goal is shalom—that is, whole, healthy relationships between God and humans, among humans, and between humans and the earth. This shalom is portrayed in images as varied as the wolf dwelling with the lamb; swords beaten into plowshares and spears into pruning hooks and no one learning war anymore; enjoying the kind of safety that allows persons to sit under the fruit trees they much earlier planted; turning the other cheek; going the second mile; enjoying a heavenly city that has come down to earth in which there is food, water, medicine, and safety for all, and God is so close that no temple is needed (e.g., Isa 2:4; 65:21–22; Matt 5:39–46; Rev 21:22, 25; 22:1–2).

And at the end, the Bible affirms that "the home of God is among mortals" and that Christ is "making all things new" (Rev 21:3, 5). The goal is a city; this is an important reaffirmation of community.

Along the way, the biblical story recognizes the many ways in which things can go wrong. Not very far into Genesis, the first murder occurs. Families are disrupted by jealousy. The gift of sexuality is misused. Before long, God needs to start over, but the people selected to bless the world keep forgetting and failing to live into the desired relationship with God, each other, and the world. They long for a king, even though it is a costly path to security. And the people who had themselves been delivered from slavery are soon enslaving others.

Our faith has to do with seeing oneself as part of this larger story, with all its hope for humans and all its tragedy. The priorities of the story shape the aspirations of people of faith. The tragedies shape their resiliency. And God's generous willingness to involve humans and God's amazing respect for their freedom and responsibility undergird their sense of agency. They are called and empowered to care for the world.

Faith, as practiced by American Christians and Jews over many years, has affected our civic and political involvement in at least two ways: it shapes that to which we Christians and Jews aspire, and it deepens our wisdom—that is, our understanding of humans (how they function and what they need to live a full life) and our understanding of communities (how they function and what they need to be healthy).

So for example, religious faith, as inspired by Christian and Jewish beliefs (and increasingly by Muslim beliefs, and to some degree, by other religions), aspires to the following:

- that all people be treated justly
- that all people be treated with dignity and have their freedom respected
- that all people experience the benefits of a deeply connected community
- that all people have hope
- that all people who suffer have someone to "be with" them
- that all people have access to the basic necessities of food, shelter, education, and health care, and a meaningful role in their communities
- that empathy for others informs everyone's decision-making

These aspirations influence the political priorities of people of faith. There is room for spirited disagreement about various ways to achieve these goals, so any attempt to tie faith exclusively to one particular strategy dislocates the relationship of faith to public policy. Thus we need to remember that when it comes to humans, faith—as inspired by our Christian and Jewish scriptures—recognizes

- that we exhibit an amazing ability to deceive ourselves and fail to recognize when self-interest intrudes;
- that we are always "on the way" with yet more to learn;
- that tribalism threatens to undermine genuine communities;
- that political power is both useful and dangerous;
- that polarization yields either conflict or paralysis;
- that fear, though useful in the face of real danger, can readily undermine the bonds that hold us together and enable us to pursue the common good; and
- that engaged diversity strengthens a community.

Historians have noted that almost every significant positive social change that has occurred in America has been instigated and/or supported by faith communities and religious leaders. This is true, for example, in ending the slave trade, in starting schools and colleges on the frontier, in leading the civil rights movement, in opposing nuclear weapons, and in supporting environmental stewardship. In the 1980s, when the place of nuclear weapons was under intense discussion, one of my (Darrell's) colleagues, Professor William Jennings, was leading a semester-long program in Washington, DC, for students from several church-related colleges. The program included a reading seminar, internships, interviews of governmental office holders, and visits with staff members of social service projects. Dr. Jennings described a phone call he had had with a member of the Defense Department, seeking a security clearance for the students to visit there. He said there should not be a problem because this was a church group. The response: "A church group! They're the ones giving us all the trouble!" The security clearance was issued without any problem, but it was reassuring to learn that, even in the Pentagon, the witness of the church regarding nuclear weapons was being noticed.

Observers of American society have noted the critical role that faith groups have played in fashioning our country's social and civic life. The French diplomat Alexis de Tocqueville, after traveling around America, observed in his 1835 book *Democracy in America* that religion was the first of America's "political institutions" where people learned to practice democracy.[14] Robert Putnam, famous for his essay on "Bowling Alone" that warned that Americans were becoming too individualistic, later wrote a book with the same title. In it he appealed to faith communities as "the single most important repository of social capital."[15] What he meant by "social capital" is the trust that develops from regular face-to-face gatherings. This trust is what enables a community to work together, deal with a crisis, and make necessary changes.

Throughout the first two centuries of America, religious organizations—primarily Protestant, Catholic, and Jewish—used this social capital to serve not only their own members but society at large through the establishment of educational, health, social service, and philanthropic institutions. A list of such institutions would fill several pages of this book. A few examples include Seventh Day Adventist, Catholic, and Jewish hospitals; Methodist, Lutheran, Baptist, and Jesuit colleges; Quaker, Baptist, and Lutheran disaster relief organizations; and Jewish philanthropies. It is worth noting that Lutheran Services in America, representing over three hundred Lutheran nonprofits, is the largest social service network in the country even though Lutherans number less than 3 percent of the population.

Special mention should be made concerning the role of the Black church in our American history. The African Methodist Episcopal Church, Black Baptist churches, and other predominantly Black denominations and congregations have served as ongoing places of community support for Blacks during times of crisis, terror, sadness, and celebration. They have given leadership to bring about desperately needed changes through the civil rights movement of the 1950s, 1960s, and beyond. They have continued to foster hope in the face of ongoing racist structures and policies in our society. They have been a source of strength, organization, education, and inspiration in local neighborhoods throughout the country. As a result, our entire society continues to benefit from their active presence and leadership.

Our Christian and Jewish faiths have been expressed and continue to be expressed in a variety of meaningful ways throughout the American landscape. They continue to be powerful forces for good.

THE PROMISE OF RELIGIONS NEW
TO AMERICAN SOCIETY

On April 19, 1995, two revengeful Americans executed the tragic bombing of the Murrah Federal Building in Oklahoma City, killing more than 160 people. The press originally put out false reports that accused people from "Middle Eastern groups" of being responsible for the attacks, sparking a number of anti-Muslim violent incidents around the country. The media soon corrected this false reporting. But when the press later covered the rescue and humanitarian aid responses, what they failed to mention was that Muslim firefighters were actively involved in the immediate rescue efforts, Muslim doctors treated and helped save the lives of many of the injured in the city's hospitals, and Muslim organizations gave substantial time and financial donations in the follow-up efforts to help the families impacted by the tragedy.[16] Indeed, Americans are often not aware of the important charitable and humanitarian efforts of Muslims, Buddhists, Hindus, Sikhs, and others representing the "religions new to American society." The following brief descriptions of several of these religions provide an introduction to their core beliefs, but most importantly, indicate through examples how they are using the power of their faiths for the good of all Americans.

Muslims. As a result of the attacks of 9/11 and the violence of ISIS and others, Islam is often totally misrepresented to the American public. The five pillars of Islam are a confession of faith, prayer, fasting, charity, and a pilgrimage to Mecca. Charity plays an important role in the Islamic faith. Much like Christians, Muslims are encouraged to regularly give a percentage of their assets to benefit others. Charitable donations go to help other Muslims in need in America and beyond, but they often benefit non-Muslim people and institutions as well. We have already noted the many times that Muslim leaders have responded with personal help and donations when Christians and Jews have suffered from violent acts of prejudice and bigotry.

Contrary to reports sometimes circulating on social media, Islam does not have a goal to make everyone a Muslim. Reza Aslan, in his comprehensive book about Islam, points out that Islam "has had a long commitment to religious pluralism," beginning with Muhammad's recognition of Jews and Christians as "protected people."[17] This expected toleration of other religions is summarized in one important verse in the Qur'an: "Let there be no compulsion in religion" (2:256).[18] We have noted that in some Islamic countries, this call for appreciation of religious diversity has been replaced by the misuse of religion for political control and power. American Muslims are seeking to overcome this abuse of religion in foreign countries by participating actively in interfaith efforts and organizations here in America that promise and seek to support religious freedom.

Muslims in America come from a wide variety of national backgrounds and from a diversity of groups within Islam, including the Sunni, Shiite, and Wahhabi divisions. In America, they have created a number of organizations designed to bring these diverse Muslims together and help them find an active role in the social and civic life of their new nation. These include the Council on American Islamic Relations, the Islamic Society of North America, and the Council on Islamic Education. These national organizations are often supplemented by local and regional ones. For example, in the San Francisco Bay area, a group of young Muslims has created an organization called AMILA (American Muslims Intent on Learning and Activism). Their goal is to be "fully involved in community and service activities, both for Muslims and for the wider society."[19] This goal is a very positive sign of "the power of faith for good."

Though *Buddhists* practice a religion without the same sense of having a "supreme being" as is found in Islam, Christianity, and Judaism, the religion of Buddhism has had a growing impact on American society. The teachings of the Buddha, who lived more than twenty-five hundred years ago in Northern India, were known as Dharma. These teachings seek to move people from "suffering" to freedom and enlightenment through meditation, insight, and ethical behavior.

Buddhists have arrived on American soil from a wide variety of Asian countries, including Thailand, Cambodia, Vietnam, Korea, China, Japan, Tibet, and Sri Lanka. As a result, a great deal of variety is found in Buddhist temples and practices, as Buddhists seek to preserve cultural identity and contribute to American society at the same time. Based on the original teachings of the Buddha, many Buddhists believe they can make special contributions to America's future through their teachings about peacemaking, preserving our environment, and physical and spiritual healing.[20]

Buddhists are also finding special ways to link with people of other religions. Each year in June, for example, the Kurukulla Center for Tibetan Buddhist Studies in Medford, Massachusetts, conducts its Saka Dawa interfaith celebration, inviting people from a variety of faiths throughout the greater Boston area to come together to share, celebrate, and develop wider friendships.

Hindus have clearly had a meaningful impact on many Americans, especially over the past half-century. We are familiar with a variety of names that have emerged from the various beliefs and practices of Hinduism, including yoga, mind-body clinics, the Maharishi and Transcendental Meditation, holistic health, and the teachings of gurus.

Hinduism, often called the "world's oldest religion," had its origins in India not with one teacher but with a variety of religious philosophies that began to be collected in oral and written form over many centuries before and after the fifth century BCE. The main scriptures include the Vedas and the Bhagavad Gita—the "Song of God"— that express pathways of contemplation and wisdom, devotion, and ethical actions. Hinduism points to God and the divine but under a variety of names—Shiva, Vishnu, and Ganesha—whose images appear in a variety of temples found in communities throughout the American landscape.

Hindus continue to practice their religion while seeking to find their place in America's multireligious society that values freedom of religion. Recently, many Hindus have been concerned about the attempts in India to infuse Hinduism into the country's national political life, with some Indian Hindus calling for a "Hindu nation." This situation brought controversy to the 2018 World Hindu Congress, held in Illinois. In response, Nitika Sharma, spokeswoman for the congress, released a public statement declaring that diversity of religious thought is "one of the core values of Hindu dharma" or teaching.[21]

American Hindus—with this respect for religious diversity in their own faith and among other faiths, their spiritual teachings that encourage the development of healthy minds and bodies, and their ethical concerns—believe that they can be a positive force for our country. As Hindus continue to enter into the arenas of science, medicine, and public life, they can use the power of their faith for good.

The *Sikhs* in America practice a monotheistic religion that originated in the Punjab region of India in the fifteenth century CE. Though Americans are less familiar with Sikhism, it is the world's fifth-largest organized religion. Its belief system is based on the spiritual teachings of the first Guru, Guru Nanak. The holy scripture of the Sikhs is the Guru Granth Sahib, a volume of poetic composition that envisions people living in a society of justice and without oppression.

Sikh beliefs fit well with the goals of America's democratic society. The sacred scriptures of the Sikhs call for unity and equality for all of humankind, striving for justice and prosperity for all, and encouraging Sikhs to engage in selfless service. A recent example from Oceanside, California, describes a Sikh couple taking seriously these scriptural callings. Davinder Singh and his wife, Harisimran Kaur Khalsa, witnessed the hunger of local people living in a park in Oceanside. They began raising money to purchase a trailer so they could take food to needy people not just in the park but throughout the surrounding county. To support their service to others, they created the Duwara Consciousness Foundation, not only to provide hunger relief, but also to teach compassion for others and to promote equality. Singh explained their commitment with these words: "We have a lot of friends who are from different faiths, and in all honesty, it's in all of our faiths to help others."[22]

Sikhs demonstrated the call of their faith to help others in special ways during the coronavirus pandemic. In suburban Detroit, for example, Shalinder Singh and his children, Arjun and Baani, delivered thousands of pizzas, paid for by Singh, to frontline workers in hospitals, police stations, and fire departments. Carrying out a key tenet of his faith to help others through "langar," a communal meal shared by all who come, Singh said he did so because it was "time to take care of the heroes on the front."[23] These Sikh approaches to a life of serving others certainly demonstrate the power of faith for good!

These six faiths referenced above—Christianity, Judaism, Islam, Buddhism, Hinduism, and Sikhism—are the largest in numbers in our multireligious America. There are others found in communities throughout America, including Confucianism (considered by many as more of a philosophy than a religion), Jainism (a nontheistic religion founded in India), the Baha'i faith, Zoroastrianism, and the Native American tribal religions, the first religions on our continent. Some Native Americans practice Christianity while still participating in their tribal religious ceremonies. The Native American emphasis on caring for sacred places on our earth reminds all Americans of the environmental concerns we face now and into the future.

UNIVERSAL NORMS

As we have described, religions are not the same. Their differences are often quite significant. But this does not mean that they have nothing in common. Religions all seek to foster some type of moral standards. Many people will still believe that their faith has the "right answers," but in a democracy, a particular moral standard can be discussed and contested as people seek to find commonalities. As Michael Ignatieff has articulated in his book *The Ordinary Virtues*, the goal is to "universalize the norm, already proclaimed in the world's great religions, that all human beings have a protected moral status."[24] He emphasizes that "religious languages of human universality in general are the oldest, and they may prove to be the most enduring vernacular in which human beings recognize their common identity."[25] Ignatieff has searched among various ethnic groups with a variety of faith beliefs and practices and has found among them common "ordinary virtues," including trust, tolerance, forgiveness, and reconciliation.

One function of interreligious engagement is to identify our commonalities so that the various faith communities can work together to foster the common good. Our commonalities can often be discovered in surprising ways. A recent book, with essays from eight different faith perspectives, reveals that the concept of vocation—of a calling to serve the neighbor and the community in whatever way possible—finds support in Judaism, Islam, Buddhism, Hinduism, Confucianism, and Christianity.[26] I (Darrell) heard four of the authors from the book speak about their participation in the project. Each said their initial reaction had been to doubt that "vocation" was supported by their religion because the word was not employed there. But when they dug deeper, they were amazed at the degree of overlap. In each religion, they found a basis for affirming and practicing one's vocation—a calling to serve the neighbor and the community. Other areas of possible overlap are the shared goal of peace and the importance of caring for the poor.

WORKING TOGETHER FOR THE COMMON GOOD

Interfaith dialogue can and should lead to interfaith action for the benefit of all people in our society. When religious organizations work together, they can become powerful forces for the common good.

Interreligious networks are emerging at national and local levels. The North American Interfaith Network (NAIN) brings together representatives of interfaith councils from the United States, Canada, and Mexico. People of a wide variety of faiths connect through both on-site major gatherings and digital conferencing. The Interfaith Conference of Metropolitan Washington is a great example of an active local interfaith organization. Its membership includes the following: Buddhists, Baha'is, Mormons, Hindus, Jains, Jews, Muslims, Protestants, Roman Catholics, Sikhs, and Zoroastrians. The conference describes its mission as creating "an inclusive community of diverse faiths in our nation's capital that is focused on values that unite us and the distinctions that can make each faith unique."[27] Highlighted programs are an annual Unity Walk that includes both interfaith dialogue and service projects, a project in honor of Rev. Martin Luther King Jr. to build homes for the homeless, and an Interfaith Leadership Summit to help get younger people involved.

Deep concern for the humane treatment of refugees and especially for the well-being of refugee children represents a powerful example of leaders of various faiths coming together for the common good. In response to children dying on our southern border while in US detention, Rev. Elizabeth Eaton, presiding bishop of the Evangelical Lutheran Church in America, invited religious leaders to craft a widespread interfaith response that said in part, "We urge the Administration to maintain its commitment to international law and defend human rights by implementing safeguards to ensure the safety and health of all of those seeking protection in our land, especially those children who fall under our care." The statement was signed by representatives of seventeen Christian, Jewish, and Islamic denominations, along with three major ecumenical councils.[28] Our country will be much improved when people of many faiths come together to challenge us to live up to our moral and legal obligations.

The state of Minnesota has long been noted as the "Land of 10,000 Lakes," but in recent years, people from all over the world are also motivated to come to the state to visit and shop at the Mall of America in Bloomington. Recognizing the diversity of people who come to this giant facility, the mall has created the Mall Area Religious Council (MARC). Founded in 1992, MARC's mission is to "provide an interfaith presence at the Mall of America in promoting mutual recognition and understanding among all peoples and religions, while fostering cooperation, meaning, compassion, and peace in our conflicted world."[29] Each November, MARC sponsors a "Peace Walk and Holy Days and Holidays of Thanksgiving around the World."

Another growing interfaith effort has arisen out of concern for the future of the planet we all share. Interfaith Power and Light, a national organization with currently forty state affiliates, was created to inspire and mobilize "people of faith and conscience to take bold and just action on climate change."[30] Active programs include an annual Faith Climate Action Walk to encourage a clean energy future and a Cool Congregation program to encourage local congregations to be more energy efficient in their own facilities and communities.

Interfaith organizations can make a real difference in our political system as well, at local, state, and national levels. An interfaith joint witness has power because the politicians who are charged with finding the appropriate way to accomplish what needs to be done are far more likely to listen to a multifaith recommendation than a request from an individual faith community. There are at least two reasons for this. One is to avoid violating the first amendment. The other reflects the likelihood that a multifaith recommendation is oriented to the common good rather than the interests of a single group.

To be sure, all religions have made major mistakes over the years in not carrying out the best callings of their faiths. But change does not come by people merely adopting certain "spiritual thoughts" that can indeed be helpful to individual lives. Change requires collective action. And religious organizations, including local congregations, still provide great opportunities for mobilizing caring people to bring about important change in our society, including the embracing of religious and racial diversity. And when various religions work together, they greatly enhance "the power of faith for good."

CHAPTER SIX

Embracing Racial and Religious Diversity

A Critical Focus for Our Calling—Our Vocation

We all can rejoice in recognizing the power of faith for good. Now we must ask these fundamental questions: Where do we go from here? How can each of us be inspired to do what we as Christians are called to do? The answer, we believe, comes with understanding the nature of our Christian vocation and, with God's help, responding to this vocational call by striving for a more loving, just, and joyful life for us all.

In this chapter, we will unpack the concept of vocation and tie it to the critical issues that lie before us. Vocation helps inspire and guide our behavior in all areas of life. This calling includes embracing racial and religious diversity in our lives and in our country.

This chapter provides a pivotal point for the book. It seeks to draw together, around the concept of vocation, some ideas already introduced in earlier sections and augment them with other proposals. The concept of vocation then provides the basis for the practical suggestions in the following two chapters.

Christian vocation is fundamentally a calling to love and serve the neighbor and the community. For the sake of clarity, distinguishing "vocation" from "occupation" is critically important. Several years ago, I (Darrell) heard a rabbi speak. He described a recent move that his family had made. Two or three movers arrived at their home, packed up all their belongings, loaded them in a truck, hauled them to their new home, and unpacked them. All of this took three or four days. Throughout it all, the rabbi noticed that one of the movers was especially helpful. At the end, before he left, the rabbi mentioned to him what he had observed and asked him about himself. The mover replied, "Moving is a very stressful time for a family. My vocation is to help families deal with that stress." His occupation was moving furniture and other belongings; his vocation was helping families deal with stress.

Not only are vocation and occupation not the same, but a robust sense of vocation can call into question an occupation. If making a particular product, a person with a robust sense of vocation asks, "Who is benefitting from this product? Is anyone being harmed by its use? Is the process of making it doing any harm?" The answers to those questions determine whether making this particular product can be both an occupation and a vocation. An example of how an occupation and a vocation may not overlap is in the case of a German train engineer during the 1940s. Even if he did his job and did it well, while never asking who the people on the train were and what would happen to them at Auschwitz, his work contributed to the Holocaust, a mass murder. His vocation should have challenged his occupation.

Vocation knows no boundaries. We all live in such an interconnected world that a person's individual decisions affect not only one's coworkers, not only one's family, not only one's neighborhood, but also persons in many other parts of the world. What an individual American contributes to global warming affects droughts and food production in Africa and Central America. What a citizen says about immigration directly affects refugees hoping to find asylum in the United States. Where a person decides to vacation affects employment and taxes and other living conditions in tourist areas here and abroad. Contributions to a relief organization directly affect the well-being of those served by that organization—be they in Sudan or Haiti or Ethiopia or Nepal.

Since vocation knows no boundaries, it deserves a fuller definition. A sense of vocation involves the realization that, as a human being, I am not an isolated unit but am nested in a larger community and that my highest moral responsibility is so to act in all areas of my life as to benefit that community and the individuals in it.

As we discussed in chapter 2, at least two essential ingredients foster and support a robust sense of vocation. One is a sense of gratitude that, in its most profound meaning, begins with thankfulness to God for God's generosity, many gifts to us, and readiness to restore our relationship with the divine. But all of us, including those who do not recognize God, can acknowledge that we did not choose to be born, we did not care for ourselves when we were infants, and we did not build the schools that we attended or do anything to merit whatever good teaching we experienced. Even though we may contribute to their upkeep, we did not build the roads on which we drive or plant the trees that grace our landscape. Every one of us has benefitted from mentors or advocates. And even those things for which we tend to be given credit are indirectly gifts from others. If we did well in school, who taught us to value education? If we have been industrious, who taught us to work hard? The truth is, we are interdependent. An essential ingredient in vocation is acknowledging this interdependence and allowing gratitude for it to influence our behavior. What do we do with this gratitude? The idea of vocation is to "pass it forward" to others.

The second essential ingredient is the "call" of the other—a lively recognition that someone needs help or that, for the sake of our neighbor, something needs changing. To some extent, vocation comes from within a person, but in a still deeper sense, we are drawn into it from outside ourselves—by the needs of another person or group of persons. Sharon Parks and her colleagues examined one hundred individuals from various parts of the United States and from various backgrounds, all of whom were particularly active in their neighborhoods and communities. Parks's team wondered what these otherwise diverse individuals had in common. Most of what they discovered did not surprise them. These individuals who were active in their communities had had mentors and models. They had benefitted from a relationship in which they found a safe place to consider alternatives. Many had been influenced by their religious traditions. But Parks and her colleagues did not expect one similarity that stood out. All of the one hundred individuals had had an experience or series of experiences of crossing over a social boundary and sensing the humanity of those on the other side. As the authors observed, "The single most important pattern we have found in the lives of people committed to the common good is what we have come to call *a constructive, enlarging engagement with the other.*"[1] For this to happen, "some threshold had been crossed, and people had come to feel a connection with the other."[2] One example of this was a woman who, as a church member, visited a nearby prison. As she returned and learned to know the inmates, she gradually came to see the prisoners as humans who needed education and counseling in order to prepare them to "make it" once they were released. She started what has become a large program of classes and counseling. For another, the "other" was someone with a disability or mental illness. Or someone of a different race. Or someone who was hungry. Or someone who had fought on the other side in a war. The list could go on, but in every case, what was crucial was experiencing the humanity and the needs of the "other." This recognition and these needs drew these hundred people into a deep sense of vocation and helped them focus on how it would be lived out. Not only is a "constructive, enlarging engagement with the other" crucial for eliciting a keen sense of vocation in general; it is also crucial for constructing a vocational commitment to interracial and interreligious relations.

We believe that this framework of vocation offers the most powerful way to build a more just society—one that recognizes the dignity of persons of different races and religions. A sense of vocation compels us to address these critical questions: What are we called to do individually? What are we called to do along with others in our congregations and our communities? And how does our calling help guide our way?

Our answer includes the following aspects of our vocation today, each of which will be examined more closely in the sections that follow.

WE ARE ALL CALLED TO "SEE" OTHERS

First, an image: A few years ago, St. Olaf College gave an honorary degree to a man from overseas who had attended the college, returned to his home country, and served in an important position there. In his brief acceptance speech, this man said that the chief gift he had been given during his time at the college was that for the first time in his life he was "seen." What he likely had in mind was that he was viewed primarily not as a member of a family or a member of a social or economic class but as an individual with dignity and worth. He was highlighting an important dimension of vocation. Any barrier—racial, religious, or national—can prevent us from "seeing" others. Stereotypes can get in the way. Our calling is to "see" others and to value them. To "see" them also means to listen to their stories. Indeed, "seeing" is one of the most valuable gifts we can give to those who are considered "not one of us."

My (Darrell's) father espoused a simple, down-home philosophy with significant implications: "Everyone puts their pants on one leg at a time." For him, this meant everyone was to be treated with respect, no matter what their social status. They were to be "seen." It also meant that he expected everyone to have an interesting story and was always on the lookout for something he could learn from talking with them. He was as interested in talking with a local farmhand as with a seminary student from Ethiopia, as interested in talking with a neighborhood teenager as with a former senator in his home in a Washington, DC, suburb or a graduate professor at Yale.

His approach to others reflected the Christian claim that everyone is created in the image of God. We are called to "see" that image in everyone we meet.

WE ARE CALLED TO SEE OURSELVES DIFFERENTLY

When it comes to race, we are called to be out of step with the social arrangements of our day. As we discussed in chapter 4, this means for white Christians and others that we are called not only to listen carefully to people of color in order to learn about their experience, which is usually quite different from our own, but also to see ourselves differently. To repeat, white Christians have too often assumed that the experience of people of color is the same as ours when it is not. We have correctly perceived that in many ways we are generous and open but without noticing the limits of these qualities—namely, our thoughtless participation in the racial hierarchy of this country. We have assumed that it is up to people of color to overcome whatever disadvantages racism thrusts upon them. We need to see that our contentment with the status quo is part of the problem. In other words, we need to repent—that is, "to turn around," to turn away from the racist assumptions we have internalized from our society and turn toward another way.

This other way can be found in the Scriptures, where race as we know it is not an issue but where social inequities are taken seriously—by the God of creation, by the God of Exodus, by the prophets, and by Jesus. Again and again, the Scriptures hold up the ideal of a world of just, caring, healthy, and equitable relationships. People of faith are equipped with a vision of what can be and with the grace to practice it.

A compelling reason for white Christians (and others) to recognize and work to overcome structural racism in our society is that the barriers need to be challenged from both sides of the racial divide. If white Christians do not work to make changes and work to convince other white Americans to join their efforts, the result will be increased conflict and the risk of even more stringent barriers for people of color. In the face of changing demographics, the status anxiety of many white Americans could, unfortunately, prompt them to support policies of discrimination—in voting, in the justice system, in education, in housing, and in job opportunities. We must dismantle racism and make sure that these results never come to pass!

Every human has been created in the image of God, and God's generosity is available to all. This generosity equips us to listen, to seek to understand, and to stand with our neighbors of every color and religion.

WE ARE ALL CALLED TO BE ENGAGED WITH OTHERS

Why engagement? We have already heard from Robert Putnam, whose sociological analysis laments the decline in regular face-to-face meetings because those meetings build trust and build the "social capital" needed for a community to make changes and handle a challenge. The strength of a community depends on members who are engaged with each other.

Additionally, those who work with groups to reduce prejudice of any kind—ethnic, racial, religious, cultural—have learned that exposure is not enough. By itself, exposure can often be counterproductive. It can increase each group's misperception of the other. Interpersonal engagement is needed in order to challenge the stereotypes people carry, recognize the social patterns that affect their own outlooks and behaviors, and acknowledge their commonalities.

Engagement is important for another reason—to overcome isolation. The isolation of one group from another produces misunderstandings, and these misunderstandings lead to fear. Self-appointed agitators then build on this fear to make things worse for those who are "not one of us."

WE ARE ALL CALLED TO BUILD RELATIONSHIPS
BY MEANS OF GENEROSITY AND HOSPITALITY

If a restored God-human relationship is built on generosity and hospitality, the same is true of every healthy human-to-human relationship. When our parents nurtured us while we were as yet unable to help ourselves or assist them, their generosity was building a relationship. When a particularly influential teacher showed a special interest in us, that teacher's generosity was building a relationship within which we could grow and learn. When a friend goes out of his or her way to help us, that person's generosity is strengthening the bonds of friendship. Every healthy human-to-human relationship is built on generosity.

Generosity does not first assess the qualities of the other person to decide whether that person is "worthy" of affection or friendship. Generosity goes to work, seeking to build a connection. Yes, to be sure, the other person can sabotage the process. Instead of responding with grace, the other can inflict the kind of emotional or physical wounds that jeopardize the growth of trust. But this occasional outcome does not change the truth that generosity yields trust, and that trust is at the heart of a healthy relationship.

If all personal relationships are built on generosity, then this is also true of interreligious and interracial relationships. How can each of us build a good relationship with a person of another faith? Unless dealing with an extremist, we do not need to first assess the virtues or shortcomings of another religion in order to treat the practitioner of that religion well. Our calling is to begin with generosity and hospitality. Our calling is to seek to understand that person, including the role that religion plays in that person's life.

WE ARE ALL CALLED TO *BE* NEIGHBORS, TO SERVE AND BE SERVED

We are called to *be* neighbors. Recall that in Luke 10, in answer to the lawyer's question, "Who is my neighbor?" (Luke 10:29), Jesus tells the story of the Good Samaritan and asks Who "do you think was a neighbor?" (Luke 10:36) Our calling is to *be* a neighbor to those on the other side of today's social barriers.

How can each of us be a good neighbor to a person of another race? Unless we have significant interaction with them, we cannot know what they have experienced. Without this insight, we cannot assess in advance their character. We need to make room for the other person to defy our preexisting stereotypes. And we have to take into account the possibility that persons of another race have had the kind of bad experiences that make them reluctant to build this new relationship. We may have some general information before the relationship begins, but we cannot know without listening how that person has experienced racial differences.

Discussions of our vocation, our calling to serve the neighbor and the community, often focus on what we can do for others. This perception is appropriate but incomplete. Interreligious and interracial relationships often exhibit some mutuality. For example, they entail learning from the other. In order for this to take place, our neighbor of a different race or religion typically shows some generosity toward us. It would be possible for them not to be bothered. It would be possible for them not to take the risk. Every year during the 1990s, I (Darrell) invited Judy Freeman, a Holocaust survivor, to speak to one of my classes. The Nazis had put her in a concentration camp when she was fourteen. With the help of friends from her hometown, she made it through the ordeal. When asked once if it was painful for her to tell her story, she said yes; it was painful every time. But she continued to do it, not only for our class, but also for middle school and high school students. Though she did not use the word, she did it out of a sense of vocation. She did it for the sake of the students, hoping they would be challenged to make a difference in the world. It was, as we have been saying, an act of generosity. For her and for others, allowing us to see life through their eyes is a gift. Yes, we may at first feel challenged by a different way of perceiving the world and challenged by an outsider's view of our own race or religion, but in the long run, these too can be gifts. Being a neighbor often involves a gracious receiving—in some cases, receiving even what is difficult for them to say or for us to hear.

The call to serve the neighbor may entail helping another person. But it is important that "serve" is not always an "inclined plane" relationship where someone with more means is helping someone with fewer. More often than not, the relationship that works best develops into one that is reciprocal, where persons work together to find solutions. This understanding is especially important in interracial relationships because people of color have already experienced what it is like to be denied the privileges society bestows on whites.

The playing field needs to be leveled so that people on both sides of a racial divide can work together to change the social pressures and policies that divide them. Understanding that a reciprocal relationship is important also applies to interreligious relationships. In the United States, a person who practices another religion already experiences what it is like to live in a society that has, for example, been shaped by the Christian calendar. People of differing religions need to work together to address the impediments to full participation for all. In the process, they often discover they have more in common with each other than they do with secularists who dismiss the importance of religion and religious ethics.

WE ARE ALL CALLED TO LEARN MORE

We are all called to learn more—about others and about ourselves. Learning more about the religion practiced by our neighbor is an important part of understanding that person. Valuable learning can come from both person-to-person dialogue and study about that religion (so long as the authors studied have an informed, appreciative understanding of it). Learning more about those of another race includes both person-to-person listening and reading authors who convey the experience of what it is like for them to live in our society. Learning more about ourselves involves finding ways to see ourselves as others see us. For example, persons from a Muslim community in the Middle East wonder, when they see the advertisements that come from the West, whether our society is completely secular and materialistic. And persons from any number of more communal societies notice how individualistic we are and how much we expect others to be the same. They are perplexed by our disregard for communal ties and responsibilities. When we are allowed to see ourselves in a mirror, we find ourselves facing basic questions. How should our faith influence our behavior in this kind of society? What does our faith have to say about materialism and individualism?

This call to learn more is supported by the biblical view of human origins. According to Genesis, all humans are descended from a single couple, and all—both male and female—are created in the image of God. The theological and ethical purpose of these affirmations is a reminder that we are all family. No one in another religion or in another race can be excluded or regarded to be subhuman. According to Rabbi Shai Held, "In ancient Near Eastern societies, it was the king who was thought of as an image of God: it was he who was appointed to rule over others and to mediate God's blessings for them. Genesis 1 will have none of this. It is not the king who is the image of God but each and every human being, male and female (Gen 1:26–28). Genesis 1 issues a breathtaking call to place human worth and dignity at the very center of worlds both public and private."[3]

The kinship of all humans seems to be confirmed by contemporary science, which identifies very little genetic difference (about 0.1 percent) between persons of one skin color and those of another. It is thus no surprise that numerous attempts during the nineteenth and early twentieth centuries to locate measurable differences in the biological traits of various races failed quite dramatically. Unfortunately, neither Genesis nor science has been able to reshape our society's perception of racial differences.

If every human is this similar, and if in God's eyes every human has dignity, then we need to recognize our human ties and be ready to learn from others. This learning will expand and deepen our understanding of what it means to be human and our capacity to act in ways that genuinely benefit those around us.

WE ARE ALL CALLED NOT TO BEAR FALSE WITNESS AGAINST OUR NEIGHBOR

Martin Luther's explanation of the commandment against bearing false witness begins in a way one would expect. He says, "We should not tell lies about our neighbor, nor betray, slander, or defame him [or her]." But he does not stop there. He goes on to find in the commandment a positive recommendation: that we should speak well of our neighbor and put the most positive construction on all that our neighbor says and does. How does Luther's explanation relate to the call to embrace diversity? Allowing ourselves to hold and pass along stereotypes about persons in another race or those who practice another religion is a violation of this commandment. Not only that, but this commandment calls us to go farther, to assess the ideas and actions of others with generosity.

Given the loaded rhetoric that swirls around today, we need to be particularly careful about being deliberately misled. One example is (mis)quoting from the Qur'an to claim that Islam is a religion of violence when in reality the quotations endorse defensive actions. Historically, Islam spread by following the trade routes more than by conquest. We should recognize that Christianity has been at least as much "a religion of conquest" as Islam. For example, the conquest of the Americas was justified by the pope when he authorized European powers to claim any land not ruled by Christians. An example of a deliberately misleading expression, this time from the civil rights era in US history, was the use of "quality education" to signal non-integrated, predominately white schools. More recently, an example of stereotyping is the frequent use of "illegal immigrants" to refer to everyone coming across our southern border, when in fact the term does not apply to a large number of current immigrants. As a party to an international treaty to provide asylum for persons whose life is in danger, the United States recognizes that those coming here (from Central America, for example) who step across the border and ask for asylum are here legally. This is in fact what many are doing. To that degree, the language of "illegal immigrants" is misleading. And as the term gets used and reused, as speakers urge that the borders be closed and complain about the costs of resettlement, some Americans begin to think that all immigrants, including the carefully vetted refugees fleeing war in Africa or the Middle East, do not belong here. Things get even further off track when the individuals and families who seek entry are lumped together as "criminals," "drug dealers," or even "animals." Our calling is to avoid stereotypes. Our calling is to understand how bad things were for those seeking asylum, for those who faced such threats that they chose to risk all and leave their homelands.

Language matters. How another group is portrayed makes a difference in how much we identify with them. Acts of hostility almost always begin with misleading characterizations. Our calling is to learn the truth and tell the truth. Our calling is to put the most positive construction on what the members of another group say and do. Our calling is to object to pejorative descriptions before they incite someone to take matters into their own hands and harm members of that group. We are called not to bear false witness against our neighbor.

WE ARE ALL CALLED TO REFRAIN FROM PREMATURE JUDGMENTS ABOUT ANOTHER RELIGION

In Exodus, chapter 3, Moses receives a call, a vocation, by means of a voice coming from a burning bush. He asks for the name of the God who is calling him. The voice responds, "I am who I am" (Exod 3:14) or "I will be who I will be" (authors' translation from the Hebrew). In ancient Israel, a name provided insight into the identity of another. In this case, the voice from the bush resists Moses's request for that insight and thereby forestalls any attempt to use this information to manipulate God. The voice's answer retains God's freedom and dynamism.

Some theologians, including Martin Luther, have reflected on the question of God's identity by describing God as both hidden and revealed. Even in the revelation that comes through Jesus the Christ, the prophets, and the Scriptures, God remains hidden—that is, we are not able to understand God fully. To be sure, revelation reveals God's attitude toward us and something of God's character and purpose, but not enough for us to have every question answered. One relevant biblical section is Romans 9–11, where Paul struggles with his questions about God's relation to the Jews who did not accept Jesus as the Messiah. He emphatically opposes the idea that these Jews have been rejected by God and affirms that the gifts and calling of God are irrevocable (Rom 11:1, 29). In the end, his basic question remains unanswered, and he throws up his hands in a doxology of praise: "O the depth of the riches and wisdom and knowledge of God! How unsearchable are his judgments and how inscrutable his ways" (Rom 11:33).

One of the questions for which there is no direct answer in the Bible is God's relation to those who practice another religion. Yes, there are prophetic denunciations of Canaanite fertility gods and the worship of idols, and yes, there are passages in the Gospel of John that seem exclusivist, but there is no direct word in the Bible regarding Rabbinic Judaism or Islam (both of which emerged later) or Buddhism, for example. We humans need to be cautious about claiming to know more than has been revealed. Our calling is to reach out to our neighbors in another religion and get to know how their religion affects their lives before making judgments about their faith. An assessment may need to be made, but the kind of understanding we have been describing should come first.

Premature judgments also occur when we forget that our faith is relational. The beliefs of Christianity can be understood only in terms of their effect on a relationship and/or those in the relationship. It is important that we not consider statements of belief to have an independent, nonrelational truth. If this is so in Christianity, it is even truer of other religions, in which beliefs do not play as central a role. In Judaism, for example, there is no creed to which people are expected to subscribe. The emphasis is on a "way of walking," a way to live one's life. In some forms of Native American religion, a ceremony is effective (at restoring communal harmony, for example), irrespective of the beliefs of its participants. It is a mistake to assess the beliefs or teachings of another religion without observing the role that they play in the lives of their adherents. To understand the role of religion in their lives, we need to get to know our neighbors who practice that religion. And even then, we need to be cautious about generalizing, because there is so much diversity within any religion.

For those of us who endorse "justification by grace alone," there is an added reason for caution. If there is no prerequisite for the gift of grace, then we cannot set a limit on its availability. We can acknowledge God's generosity toward us, but we have no basis on which to decide in advance that someone else is not eligible for or has not experienced God's grace. We need to listen to what they have to say.

What we are recommending is simply to be cautious. We can treat others with respect and listen to what they have to say and seek ways to cooperate without prejudging their religious views.

WE ARE ALL CALLED TO HAVE A
VISION OF WHAT GOD INTENDS

As already noted, scattered throughout the Bible are a number of images regarding what God intends for the world. These can be summarized by describing the goal as having whole, healthy relationships among humans, between God and humans, and between humans and the rest of creation. Our vocation is to act in ways that reflect and foster this vision.

One contemporary description of this vision of shalom comes from the ELCA "Declaration of Inter-Religious Commitment." It reads,

> God's vision is of a world in which humans and creation, in all their glorious diversity, live in unity, justice, and peace. In such a world, hope abounds, and fear no longer separates one person from another or one people from another. In this vision, 'justice roll[s] down like waters, and righteousness like an ever-flowing stream' (Amos 5:24) and 'the leaves of the tree [of life] are for the healing of the nations' (Revelation 22:2b). We envision a world in which God's grace and mercy are celebrated, and all of God's creatures and all of God's creation are regarded with value and treated with care.[4]

This vision of what God intends invites creativity. It provides an open-ended guideline for our vocation-oriented behavior. We are to treat our neighbors in such a way that we move the world one step closer to wholeness, to shalom. Providing a guiding vision is quite different from providing a rule book. A vision leaves room for our freedom and our good judgment. It provides flexibility. A vision also does not save us from failure—when even well-intentioned things go wrong. To minimize this failure, dedication to this vision needs to be supplemented both by information regarding the specific problem in need of attention and by wisdom—that is, an understanding of human beings and communities, how they function and react, and what they need in order to be whole.

A vision is also critically important because we need something to help us see what is wrong with contemporary society. The contrast between the vision and "what is" helps us identify where things have gone offtrack. Otherwise "what is" can appear to be perfectly normal or at least the best we can expect—as has happened in our society with racial inequity. A vision prevents us from becoming too content with the status quo.

WE ARE ALL CALLED TO HAVE A VISION OF WHAT AMERICA SHOULD BE

A vision of the promise of America—filled with freedom, equality, and justice—is informed by the biblical vision just described, but it is not the same. The vision of America needs to be a shared vision—one that is religiously inclusive and racially inclusive. It needs to emerge from a deep conversation with everyone represented. It needs to grow out of our founding ideals but also be modified by more than four hundred years of experience. Racism has been part of our society from the beginning. Christian triumphalism has poked its head up repeatedly from the very beginning, especially with regard to the treatment of Native Americans and with current anti-Judaic and anti-Islamic incidents. We need an updated vision for America.

There are too few places where a fruitful discussion regarding a shared vision of America is taking place today. Often what happens is that one group insists its vision is what everyone else's should be and the alternatives have no value. And then the group seeks to grab political power and use it to reshape laws and public policies and thereby enforce its priorities on others. Such efforts divide rather than unite. They contribute to polarization. And anything that divides, anything that feeds on fear, makes life more difficult for racial and religious minorities.

The worst example of one group insisting on its own narrow vision is white supremacy. Its vision is that America is for white Christians only. As we have said, its fear is that growing numbers of people of color (Blacks and immigrants) and people who practice another religion (especially Jews and Muslims) will make whites a minority. Less egregious but still dangerous forms of insisting on too narrow a vision occur when a group claims to embody exemplary patriotism, implying that those who disagree are unpatriotic, or when a reform-oriented group adopts a rigid ideology and allows it to alienate those it should be persuading.

This conversation about a vision for American needs to be inter-racial and interreligious. It needs to draw on the best from our past, but also be ready to admit our country's mistakes and devise a truth-ful version of our history and heritage. There are also new realities to confront, including, for example, the expectation that climate change will have a disproportional effect on those who are poor and people of color; the growing disparity between the wealthy and the middle/lower classes; the gradual erosion of America's reputation in the rest of the world; and the strange reality that the United States, with less than 5 percent of the world's population, has 25 percent of those who are in prison.

To live out our calling, American Christians need two visions to guide our conduct. One is the biblical vision of God's intent for the world. The other is an updated, moral vision of what America can be. As we said earlier, the biblical vision should inform the vision of America, not vice versa (as too often happens in some quarters today).

WE ARE ALL CALLED TO CHANGE SOCIETY

Not to work for change is, in effect, to say that society is OK as it is. But racism is not OK. It creates barriers. It disadvantages groups of people through no fault of their own. And it leaves those who benefit from the social pattern fearful of losing their place in society and susceptible to those who manipulate this fear into harmful results.

Denigration of another religion is likewise not OK. It violates freedom of religion. It creates barriers. It unnecessarily disadvantages groups of people who simply practice their faith. And it leaves Christians fearful of losing their place in society and susceptible to those who manipulate this fear into (re)actions that harm others.

In each of these two cases, practicing our vocation means contending with a social pattern (that makes it easier to go along than to resist) and with the effects of unjust public policies.

Social patterns have a significant effect on us. Though created by humans, they generate a social pressure that influences our decision-making. In some cases, this influence can be positive. Social pressure encourages us to have a job, for example. In other cases, the social pressure is evil. What we mean by "evil" is that these social patterns make it easier for individuals to do what is wrong than to do what is right, to do what is unjust than to do what is just. Racism exerts a social pressure on us all that is evil. It encourages what is unjust and causes us not to stand up for those on the other side of the racial boundary. As important as it is for individuals to treat their immediate neighbors well and to resist individually those patterns that are evil, the harmful social patterns themselves will not end unless there is social change. We are called both to adopt new patterns for our own behavior and to work for societal change. Only then will the pressure (experienced by all) to go along with the patterns and policies that disadvantage others be reduced.

Martin Luther, the first Protestant, understood that his Christian vocation included challenging and changing society. He had multiple callings (as a parent, a husband, a pastor, and so on), but at this point, two are important to highlight. The first was his call to be a teacher of the church. Most of us are familiar with his religious struggles, his intense study of the major church theologians and the Scriptures, and his breakthrough when he discovered, while studying Romans, that God's grace was an unmerited gift. As he spoke out about this, some taunted, "Are you the only one that is right?" And those in authority ordered him to be silent. What kept him going was the sense that he had been called to be a teacher of the church. To keep quiet was to betray this calling. He invited others to show him where he was mistaken, but until then, he would not be silent.

What is less well known is his second calling—to reform society. When he encountered the unjust social patterns of his day, he worked to change them. Consider the following:

- He may never have written his famous Ninety-Five Theses had he not wanted to stand with and stand up for the poor folks who were being ripped off by John Tetzel and the others who were selling indulgences. Several of the theses reflect this concern.

- When he wrote an open letter to the city councils of Germany, urging them to establish schools at public expense for all young men and women, he was challenging a social pattern that education was available only to the children of the wealthy. He wanted to level the playing field and equip everyone to learn from studying human history the wisdom that is needed to lead a community or a household.[5] So far as we know, he was the first person ever to make this proposal. It reflected a capacity to envision something different from "what is." And it had long-term consequences. The patterns of education did change.

- About 15 percent of Germans in his day were beggars. The church had taught that they were necessary because others needed to fulfill their religious obligation to give alms. That is, some people needed to be beggars in order for almsgiving to be possible. Luther imagined an alternative and came up with another innovative proposal. He worked with city councils to establish community chests. Into the chests went donations, proceeds from church lands, and certain taxes. A carefully selected group of citizens was in charge of dispersing those funds to anyone in need (and providing low-interest loans to shopkeepers). Guided by a vision of what could be, he found a way to change society.

- During the 1520s, discontent grew among the peasants. Their lot had become more difficult because the princes were demanding that rent be paid with money rather than labor or agricultural produce. A group of peasants wrote to Luther, identifying their grievances. He paid attention to their concerns, stated publicly that they were just, and then made his recommendation: negotiation. Luther used strong language to urge the princes to negotiate with the peasants.[6] This request was significant because he was asking them to defy a social pattern of their day. Princes considered it beneath their dignity to sit down at a negotiating table with a peasant! They refused, and war broke out. Luther had "seen" the peasants and tried, unsuccessfully in this case, to change society and save it from war.

Martin Luther provides a model for our calling. He listened to those who were being harmed by the social pattern, he imagined an alternative (based on the biblical vision of shalom), he proposed a way to make changes, and he went to work trying to accomplish those changes. Were his recommendations always successful? No. Were his recommendations political? Yes. He invited others to support them. In the case of the Ninety-Five Theses, he sought support from the church authorities, but when they did not listen, he worked in other ways to change the church. In the other cases, he appealed to the public and to the city councils. The circle broadened, and other leaders emerged.

John Calvin—Luther's contemporary, who has had a deep influence on the Reformed family of Protestants—led similar efforts to make social reforms as well as religious reforms in Geneva. Likewise, various popes from Leo XIII to Francis have urged Christians to support various forms of social justice.

Our calling is to advocate for those changes that benefit others—in particular, those affected by racism and religious antagonism. Specific suggestions about these changes will be offered in the final two chapters. Some changes are matters of individual behavior; others have to do with social patterns, policies, and structures. Reforming the latter requires political will.

At the basis of all of these individual and policy reforms is a change in outlook, in the way we see ourselves and each other. Here's where the church can do what few others can—bring people together, listen to each other's stories, and hold up a vision of what can be. It also can reassure people of God's presence and activity in the world and thereby overcome the anxiety and fear that are so pervasive today and are so paralyzing in the face of needed changes.

WE ARE ALL CALLED TO LIVE IN HOPE AND THE ASSURANCE OF GOD'S PRESENCE

How often the Scriptures recite divine promises such as "I will go with you" or "I will be with you"! It is hard to underestimate the importance of God's presence. We might be confused about what God is doing or what God wants us to do, but even then, God is present. To be called is slightly different from being sent out on one's own. It is to be accompanied, to be invited along with God into the world that needs healing. I (Darrell) remember how much I disliked an otherwise easy job that was my responsibility as a boy. It involved going down into the basement each evening and filling up the stoker with coal so that it could feed the furnace for the next twenty-four hours. The task was not difficult; nor did it take very long. What I hated was to go into the basement alone. This was in contrast to other chores where I could work with my father. They were often more difficult or unpleasant, but the presence of my father was an important difference. I somehow felt more like a partner. This difference is similar to the importance of God's presence as we carry out our vocation. We are called and accompanied, not sent out alone and on our own. The assurance of God's presence also fosters hope.

The United States was born in the eighteenth century. It was a time of optimism. People saw how a scientific understanding of water, steam, and pressure allowed steam engines to do the kind of work that had been backbreaking for humans. People saw how the use of experimental reason could open new doors by discovering simple natural laws and unmasking superstitions. People saw how societies could be changed to become more democratic. They came to expect "progress." They came to expect new and unforeseen benefits from the path they were already on. For cultural optimism, what is underway is expected to continue and be beneficial.

Hope is not the same as optimism. Hope can exist even when there is no evidence of progress, even when the storm clouds are dark. Hope is built on the confidence that God is present—that God is at work behind the scenes opening new possibilities and bringing good gifts to humans. Hope includes the confidence that God is fostering shalom, even when we are discouraged and confused.

In an essay on the relation of Judaism and Christianity, Rabbi Irving Greenberg wonders whether the biblical vision of the future is merely a daydream. But it is not, he says, because "hope is a dream which is committed to the discipline of becoming a fact."[7] He continues, "The covenant [between God and God's people] is the [mutual] pledge to work to realize the dream. . . . This unlimited partnership of the divine and the human is the ultimate dimension of religious calling in both traditions."

Hope is self-involving. It is associated with a calling. It yields active engagement. God's vision for the world will not be realized without our involvement.

It is possible, even likely, for those who experience the effects of racism or ostracism because of their religion, or for those who see this happen to others, to lose hope. Our calling is to share with them the gift of hope. This involves our presence, our listening and learning, and our commitment to change the social patterns that prevent others from being "one of us."

WE ARE ALL CALLED TO LEAD

Our vocation as humans involves not only treating individuals well but also serving the neighborhood and the wider community. The two are not entirely separate, of course, because anything that improves the community benefits the individuals within it. How do we do this? Serving the community begins with listening, especially to those in the wider neighborhood whose circumstances are different from ours—economically different, religiously different, racially different. The next steps involve identifying a problem that needs to be addressed, imagining a possible way to address it, and then consulting with others in such a way as to improve its chances of working. These actions lead to mobilizing people—enlisting support and organizing the supporters to implement the plan. All of this can be called vocational leadership or community leadership. It is the kind of leadership that is open to anyone—unlike "designated leadership," which requires an elected office or a title.

Someone has said that 90 percent of leadership is showing up. It is a striking way of communicating an important truth—that we need to be engaged in the community in order to serve it and help lead it. The sociologist Robert Putnam has documented the striking decrease, since the 1960s, in the number who participate in face-to-face neighborhood gatherings.[8] Our calling as Christians is to reverse this trend, to participate and encourage participation in gatherings where people in the neighborhood can get to know each other, come to trust each other, discuss the well-being of the community, and figure out a way to improve it.

Christianity does not give us a blueprint for structuring or governing or fostering a healthy community. Instead, we have been given a vision, a capacity for empathy, practical reason, imagination, and a certain degree of wisdom—and then have been invited to be creative.

WE ARE ALL CALLED TO PRACTICE
AND MODEL CIVIL DISCOURSE

Polarization is a debilitating impediment. Individuals today are often afraid to discuss a topic for fear that competing ideologies will lead only to unproductive conflict. In order to counteract this difficulty, we all need to learn the skills of civil discourse. For example, in 2018, Trinity Lutheran Church in St. Peter, Minnesota, sponsored a workshop for the broader community. Five or six participants sat around each table with a predesignated facilitator. The rules that would guide the discussion were described and illustrated by means of humorous videos. Then participants were asked to respond to a question about a controversial topic. The first step was for each person to *write* a response to the question. This was done to overcome the tendency to think about one's own response while others talk instead of listening to them. In step two, all the individuals, each in turn, read what they had written, with no opportunity for anyone else to respond. Step three involved going around again so that each person (within a time limit) could explain briefly what experiences had led them to write what they did. And then, as step four, all participants were asked (again within a time limit) to say where they were unsure or had questions about what they had written. Only then was there an opportunity to discuss the topic back and forth. The whole endeavor was aimed at slowing down the process and making room for more attentive listening and understanding. When participants were asked to assess the process, their response was overwhelmingly positive. The most appreciative comments were about step three, where people shared the experience(s) that had influenced what they said about the topic. This step was particularly effective at opening doors to better understanding. The reason to describe this workshop is not to recommend this specific process. It is only one of many. What is important is that we all need to develop the skills of participating in and leading a conversation about difficult topics in such a way that something productive may come of it. Otherwise, conversations are too easily undermined by polarized ideologies or prior misconceptions of the other.

Fear often fosters stereotypes and the hatred of persons who are unlike us. Fear often prevents positive civil discourse from taking place. Admitting fear is hard. Blaming the person or groups that we fear is far easier. It often takes a safe place to admit our fears. Generosity builds secure relationships, and secure relationships are safe places in which to challenge one's own ideas and consider others. The best antidote to fear is God's promise to be with us "to the end of the age" (Matt 28:20). That promise gives the kind of hope that overcomes fear.

A congregation is a great place to learn and practice civil discourse and to provide opportunities for others in the community to do the same.

WE ARE ALL CALLED TO BE PERSISTENT

Anything as deeply entrenched as racism and hostility against Muslims, Jews, and those who practice other religions will not be eliminated quickly. It takes persistence over time to change social expectations and social patterns.

But persistence is not the same as being bullheaded. Persistence involves constant listening, constant learning, and constant adjustments in strategy as we exercise our vocations, guided by the biblical vision of what God desires.

WE ARE ALL CALLED TO STAND UP, STAND FOR, AND STAND WITH THE EXCLUDED OR HARASSED

Standing up, standing for, and standing with the excluded or the harassed involves commitment and courage. This calling takes us out of our comfort zone. But carrying it out is crucial, not only for the well-being of the victims of social evil, but also to enhance the likelihood that the harmful social patterns will change.

The movie *Not in Our Town* tells the story of Billings, Montana. Some years ago, a white supremacist group arrived looking for recruits.

Their first act was to spray-paint derogatory slogans on a house where Native Americans lived. The painter's union volunteered their services to give the house a fresh coat of paint. Then a rock came through the window of a Jewish family's house. In response, the newspaper published a full-page menorah. As an act of solidarity, these (paper) menorahs were displayed in the windows of ten thousand homes. Then the white supremacists began standing in the back of a small Black church, arms folded—as a threatening presence. The response of the community was to fill up the pews with citizens ready to stand with (or sit with!) the Black congregation. In due time, the white supremacist group left Billings because its members had encountered citizens who stood up, stood for, and stood with those they targeted.

In this case, the cost was minimal. But when things get ugly, actions of solidarity can become costly. One thinks of the rescuers during the 1940s who hid persons targeted by the Nazis. They risked their own lives and the lives of their families (if discovered) in order to save one or more targeted persons. Or one thinks of the whites and Blacks who came to the aid of Black persons during the civil rights struggle in the 1950s and '60s. They faced angry crowds and unsympathetic police and sometimes overt acts of violence.

There are a variety of reasons this kind of action is important. Among them is that, when the action comes soon enough, it shows everyone that members of the community stand with the targeted group. It undercuts the claim made by the perpetrators of violence that *they* speak for the community. Standing up, standing with, and standing for others gives change a chance.

WE ARE ALL CALLED TO RECOGNIZE THE DIFFERENCE BETWEEN HEALTHY AND UNHEALTHY CONFLICT

Whenever there is social change, there is conflict. Change always involves loss as well as gain, and those who experience the loss are often reluctant to go along with the change. Unhealthy conflict occurs when two groups dig in their heels and fight for their short-term interests rather than for the good of the whole. Healthy conflict occurs when a cross section of people struggle together for change, rely on persuasion, and utilize nonviolent strategies to bring along those who are reluctant to give up the benefits of the existing system. Our calling is not to avoid conflict (as we are easily tempted to do) but to work to ensure that it is of the healthy variety.

WE ARE ALL CALLED TO HAVE A SENSE OF HUMOR

A focus on humor may seem like a strange addition to the discussion of our calling. It is intended to counteract a tendency among activists to develop a kind of moralism that produces new forms of separation. When this happens, rules take the place of relationships, and then voicing the "right" or "wrong" words creates insiders and outsiders.

By "a sense of humor," we mean not taking *too* seriously even matters that are very important for us and for others. If God does indeed love us generously and without requirements, then we are free not to take ourselves, our successes and failures, our actions, and even our morality and theology *too* seriously. As persons of faith, we can be flexible, we can risk failure, we can risk damaging our reputation, we can get in over our heads, and we can even risk compromising our virtue—all in order to help others—because of the freedom that comes from a relationship undergirded by God's steadfast love.

A sense of humor helps us avoid two potential problems: (1) recognizing that our calling is important avoids indifference, and (2) recognizing that it is not *too* important avoids moralism and leaves room for the spontaneity of people working and growing together.

WE ARE ALL CALLED TO LOVE OUR NEIGHBORS, EMBRACE DIVERSITY, AND ENJOY EACH OTHER

The framework of vocation has here been used to focus the responsibility we all have for the needs of our neighbors and the community.

This sense of responsibility could weigh us down, but the opportunity to connect with those of another race or another religion can also be a source of deep joy. Finding connections can be mutually delightful. Uncovering new insights and benefitting from the experiences and wisdom of others can be personally enriching. New connections and new discoveries can nourish, enrich, and encourage us all.

Pope Francis has said, "Whenever we encounter another person in love, we learn something new about God." Let us not miss the opportunity to reach out to those on the other side of racial or religious barriers, learn something new about them, and thereby also learn something new about God.

Indeed, God is calling us now to embrace and find new joy in America's growing diversity and in our expanding awareness of the diversity of the world God loves.

CHAPTER SEVEN

Mobilizing to Embrace Diversity

Where and how do we begin to live into our calling? One arena is, of course, our relationship with individuals. But societal racism and societal attitudes toward other religions require a broader response. In this chapter, we will discuss first the role of congregations and then the role of larger coalitions. In it, we turn from understanding to strategy, from theological study to moral commitment, from learning to action. We provide a list of viable options that congregations can use to live out their call to embrace diversity and build a more loving, caring, just, and supportive society. We describe a variety of local initiatives for others to consider. And we name supportive and visible actions on the part of a number of ecumenical organizations, denominations, colleges and universities, and theological seminaries.

THE POWER OF LOCAL ACTION

America's political and legislative history has shown that real change begins when people in both urban and rural settings, assembling in action-oriented groups, come together for discussion and make plans to take action. We believe that real, long-term cultural change will occur most powerfully at the local level.

And congregations are the place where action can and should start! Congregations are still the most well-organized, widespread communities where people can be mobilized for the common good, led by the call of the gospel. Because of the potential power of congregational action in community after community, no one can say, "What's the use? Nothing can be done." Faith matters! Theology matters! Justice matters! Our Christian calling matters! The people of congregations have the powerful example and the challenging words of Jesus, calling them to serve the poor, to reach out to the stranger, and to oppose the authorities in power, who too often—influenced by their privileged status—fail to seek liberty and justice for all of God's people. In this chapter, we will offer a wide variety of specific options for congregational and community action and then cite examples of great things already happening at the local level.

MOBILIZING CONGREGATIONS AND COMMUNITIES: OPTIONS FOR ACTION

The time is now for congregations to act. Congregations are called to take seriously the gospel message of God's love and our call to love our neighbors. Of course, some of our neighbors are in our families and in our congregational membership. The church is a unique place to gather in communion with others, to worship together, to learn together, and to give love and support to one another. But these important actions are only part of our larger mission, vision, and Christian vocation. We are called to participate in the mission of the church to build God's kingdom in our broken society. We are called to be strong advocates for the structural and policy changes necessary to bring about social justice and equal opportunities for all people. We are called to be active citizens, not just silent observers. We are called to use the unique organizational structures of our church to change the debilitating structures of our American society. We are called to heed Jesus's charge to serve the poor, the ill, the prisoners, the homeless, and the oppressed. We are called to love. We are called to embrace racial and religious diversity in our country. We are called to love our neighbors without exception! We are called to set an example for the world.

THE ROLE OF THE CHURCH: ALWAYS, AND ESPECIALLY NOW, IN AMERICA

Indeed, churches do not have to and should not remain silent or complicit. The church has always been called to be active and present in serving God's larger world.

From the beginning, God's goal has been a world in which all can flourish. This means having whole, healthy relationships among humans, between humans and nature, and between God and humans. This goal is reflected in the garden of Eden, in Abraham, in Moses, in Amos, Micah, Isaiah, and the other prophets, in Jesus, in Paul, and in John's book of Revelation. From the beginning, the calling of the church has been to serve this goal.

Thus our calling as members of the church is much broader than serving our local congregation. Yes, it can be helpful to usher, sing in the choir, and serve on the church council. But our primary calling is to change the world. Yes, it is essential that we serve individuals in need, but our calling is also to challenge those social forces that harm individuals. Christians who heard this call challenged and helped end slavery. Christians who heard this call challenged and helped end legal segregation. Christians today need to challenge and help change the persistent structural racism evident in our society. It is Christians (along with others) who need to challenge and help change those practices that contribute to global warming, with its increasingly harmful effects on human communities of all races and faiths. And it is Christians (along with others) who need to challenge and help change those economic forces that foster the increasing gap between the wealthy and the ordinary workers in our society. These are, in fact, not separate issues. The harmful effects of climate change and of poverty fall disproportionally on people of color.

How do we accomplish these critical changes? Does this mean that the church should be involved in politics? Yes and no. Yes, if "politics" means paying attention to those things that are harming people and then getting involved in actions that can reduce this harm. Yes, if it means seeking to change policies. Yes, if it means cooperating with those who are also willing to join in the movement for change. But no, if "politics" means consistently choosing one side in a partisan dispute and denigrating or not listening to the other side. The church is called not to endorse a political ideology, be it "left" or "right," but to help accomplish changes that benefit those who are being harmed, especially folks who are marginalized and lacking in political influence.

What then supports the church's calling? The confidence that God is at work behind the scenes, lifting up the lowly, breaking down the powerful, feeding the hungry, and sending the rich away empty (see Luke 1:52–53). The church's calling is not to go it alone in a God-forsaken world but to join with God in a long-term project to "mak[e] all things new" (see Rev 21:5). In other words, what supports the church's calling is hope—a hope that is built on God's grace and presence. If God is at work making all things new, then avoiding anything that is political is avoiding God's work in the world.

A few years back, I (Darrell) was talking with my granddaughter (who was then around eight years old) about helping the poor. Her response was, "But I don't know anyone who is poor." Unfortunately, the same could be said by many middle-class church members who associate only with other middle-class folks.

So how should the church respond? If we are middle-class American Christians, the first response is to hear the stories of those unlike ourselves. What is it like to be a person fleeing from violence and seeking asylum in America? What is it like to live on a street where gunfire routinely breaks out and you fear that those bullets will kill or injure one of your children? What is it like to work for a company, be laid off, and have to try to find a job when you are fifty-eight years old? What is it like not to have enough food for your children? What is it like to be a Hispanic born and raised in the United States by parents also born and raised here and be told to "go back where you came from"? We are called to hear the stories of our neighbors. And considering them "neighbors" rather than "strangers" or "outsiders" or "aliens" or "adversaries" is a crucial beginning.

The second response is to seek to help those whose stories we have heard—to welcome the stranger, to feed the hungry, to care for the sick, and in other ways, to care directly for those individuals in need. This response calls for the local church to organize to meet these immediate local needs.

The third response is to learn what it is that can be done not just to help individuals but to help larger numbers of people. Arthur Simon, the founder of Bread for the World, once explained why he had started that organization, which seeks to lobby Congress to fund food-aid programs in the United States and also in Africa and other parts of the world where there is need.* Simon said he had been working to assist individuals. But he came to feel like an ambulance driver rushing down to the bottom of a cliff to pick up someone who had fallen off, doing this again and again and again and again. He came to wonder whether his time would be better spent if he could build a fence at the top of the cliff to keep people from falling off. He decided to start an ecumenical project that would provide government funding to keep people from falling into hunger.

Our calling goes beyond bandaging individuals. We need to ask, Is there anything we can do to end the gunfire on the street where people live? Is there anything we can do to prevent age discrimination in hiring? Is there anything we can do to ensure everyone has access to food? Is there anything we can do to decrease anti-Hispanic animus? Is there anything we can do to reduce the harmful effects of racism? In order to answer those questions, we have to figure out the causes of the problems people are experiencing. Doing this takes learning. It takes creative proposals. It takes organizing to effect the changes that can help. It takes moving beyond our comfort zone into

---

* Darrell was in the audience for this talk.

overt advocacy. It takes facing the pushback of those quite comfortable with the status quo.

How do we make this happen? The task seems so large, and we seem so small in our local congregations and communities. What can congregations do to make a difference?

STRATEGIC ACTION STEPS

Based on our research of what congregations are already doing and our personal observations and experiences, here are a variety of areas for action and specific steps that congregations can undertake:

Organize to educate congregational members and prepare for action:

- Bring groups together to "revisit the Scriptures" in relation to racial and religious diversity; to see and hear the calls for justice, mercy, and equity by the Hebrew prophets; and to witness again the consistent identification of Jesus with the "unseen" people of his day. What does it mean when the Scriptures say, "Love your neighbor as yourself"?
- In sermons and worship services, boldly bring forth the biblical messages that call for justice and service to others and point toward the embracing of God's enriching human diversity.
- Organize groups to discuss books and articles that describe the challenge to white people and to the Christian church to understand much better the deepseated issues of racism, nationalism, white supremacy, Islamophobia, and reluctance to engage with people of other faiths. Suggested books, in addition to this book: Jemar Tisby, *How to Fight Racism* and *The Color of Compromise*; Lenny Duncan, *Dear Church*; Eboo Patel, *Out of Many Faiths*; Carolyn B. Helsel,

Anxious to Talk about It; Carol Schersten LaHurd, ed., *Engaging Others, Knowing Ourselves*; Angela Denker, *Red State Christians*; Jim Wallis, *Christ in Crisis*; George S. Johnson, *Silence Is Not the Answer*; Drew G. I. Hart, *Trouble I've Seen* and *Who Will Be a Witness?*; Isabel Wilkerson, *Caste.*

- Review congregational committee structures to make sure that one or more committees are given the charge to address issues of social justice and diversity. If none exists, create a new congregational committee on social action and social justice. Recruit people for the committee who are willing to learn, give leadership to taking action steps, and prepare recommendations for congregation-wide actions.
- Provide educational opportunities to help people understand the problems that affect people in the community so they can support appropriate remedies. Without this understanding, well-intentioned actions may have deleterious results for the people who are disadvantaged by social patterns and policies and suffer in other ways.

Make active use of regional and national resources to broaden congregational perspectives:
- Review the declarations of denominations and ecumenical groups that pertain to the church's understanding of racial matters, racism, social justice, and interfaith dialogue.
- Encourage congregational members to link with others through regional and national denominational structures to learn about effective opportunities for serving our neighbors in America and beyond.
- Get both adults and youth involved in reaching out to people of other faiths and other races through

regional and national gatherings and through organized outings to new environments that combine learning, service, and meaningful interaction with other diverse groups. Organize group trips to visit the civil rights movement museums and sites in Montgomery, Alabama; Memphis, Tennessee; Jackson, Mississippi; and the National Museum of African American History and Culture, the National Museum of the American Indian, and the Holocaust Museum in Washington, DC.

Engage in active dialogue with people of other races and religions:

- Invite people of other faiths to special adult forums and dialogue sessions in your church. Come together to tell stories to each other. Christians often do not have any real idea of the daily issues faced by our neighbors of other faiths. Hear their stories. Share your own feelings, fears, hopes, and visions.
- Invite Christians of other ethnic and racial backgrounds to adult forums and dialogue sessions in your church. Use the same technique of storytelling and spreading new insights to others. In this way, we get to both "see" and "know" people of other races and get to know ourselves better.
- Engage with people from both mainline and evangelical denominations with varying theological backgrounds to hear their points of view, learn of their fears and concerns, discuss the meaning of the gospel message of love for all, learn to dialogue in peaceful yet honest ways, and seek to find areas of common ground that can move our nation toward greater harmony.

Establish active, ongoing, meaningful partnerships with other religious and/or racial groups:

- Establish an ongoing partnership with a mosque, synagogue, or temple for ongoing learning, sharing, and joint activities for the common good in your community.
- Establish an ongoing partnership with a Christian congregation of another racial or ethnic background. Have groups from each church attend worship services and special events at the partnership church. Many rural congregations can connect with churches in metropolitan areas in less than a two-hour drive. Using modern online communication technology is another option for partner congregations to share greetings, prayers, and personal stories across the miles.
- Create an active, ongoing partnership between a predominantly Black and predominantly white congregation for interactive learning; sharing of worship, music, and preaching; and undertaking joint action for changes to overcome discrimination and racist societal policies and practices.
- Invite people of other faiths and ethnic groups to attend special events in your congregation. Encourage reciprocal invitations from Jewish brothers and sisters (e.g., Passover events) and Islamic brothers and sisters (e.g., Ramadan events).

Mobilize for local community fellowship and action for change:

- Give leadership to creating community events that bring diverse people together for discussion, sharing, social action, and good fun. Use existing community structures, partner with other churches, or use your own congregation to initiate and sponsor the community event.

- Use existing community events (annual festivals, parades, school events, and athletic events) to highlight and embrace local community diversity. Create special events with Black brothers and sisters to celebrate Juneteenth in meaningful ways. Broaden the annual ecumenical community Thanksgiving service (often sponsored by the local Ministerium or several Christian congregations) to include people of other faiths. Use the occasion to express thanks for all our blessings, including the special blessings that come from being part of a diverse community and diverse nation.

- Join with other faith groups in supporting local charity projects, including the local food shelf or shelter and food programs for homeless people or other low-income people who need support.

- Organize one or several gatherings of people from various faiths and races with representatives of the local police department to discuss areas for understanding and mutual support.

- Organize similar gatherings with representatives of the local school system. Encourage the teaching about various faiths and their practices in nonproselytizing ways in order to promote tolerance, appreciation, and understanding. Include appropriate songs and customs of various faiths and ethnic groups in school concerts and events.

- Organize a local campaign to place diversity support signs by the church and in people's yards with messages like "All are welcome here," "Hate has no place here," "Love your neighbor without exception," and "Blessed Ramadan." A goodly number of congregations have given special support for changes in racial policies by encouraging place-ments of "Black Lives Matter" signs as well.

- If none exists, work with others to create a community-wide organization, such as a diversity council or interfaith network, to promote inter-racial and interfaith relationships, social action, and celebrations. Such organizations may be long-term or short-lived within the larger goal of gaining active leadership participation by mem-bers of various ethnic and religious groups in ongoing community-wide organization and civic structures.

Mobilize for civic action to bring about needed changes in societal structures and policies:

- Organize a letter-writing campaign to specific public officials to respond to pending policy mat-ters and pending legislative actions. Take a stand in favor of those policies and legislative actions that favor the promotion of "liberty and justice for all," and take a stand to oppose those proposed actions that continue to perpetuate systems of racial inequality and discrimination against those of other faiths.
- Provide issue-oriented voter information regard-ing those policies that affect people of color, the poor, and those of other religions. Support voting rights and oppose policies and practices that seek to suppress opportunities for people to exercise their right to vote.
- Encourage people to be active citizens and to vote in local, state, and national elections and to let the needs of others influence their vote.
- Organize active lobbying to appropriate senators and representatives for the enactment of a new,

comprehensive, more welcoming, and generous immigration policy for America.

- Sponsor one or more immigrant families and provide immediate and ongoing support to help them adjust to their new environment.
- Give leadership to creating a language learning program for new immigrants coming into the community.
- Formally join and support the Poor People's Campaign by keeping informed of its national, regional, and state activities and organizing congregational and community members to participate in area activities.
- Use social media in a positive way to encourage others to give support to societal and policy changes at all levels to promote justice, change, and the embracing of diversity.
- Organize, as necessary, peaceful demonstrations in support of needed policy changes in local, state, and national governance. Use the lessons of the civil rights movement to make sure that people are trained ahead of time for conducting themselves in nonviolent and peaceful ways.

Celebrate and share the joy of diversity:
- Gather with people of other races and faiths, sharing ethnic foods, singing, dancing, and other customs to celebrate and experience the joy of diversity.
- Communicate, via social media and personal stories, the joy of diversity in order to help others overcome false ideas and personal fears of joining with others and encourage them to follow the true vision of the gospel message of love of neighbor and the real promise of America.

The reason for sharing the above list is to stimulate ideas for carrying out our Christian vocation through much-needed and meaningful action steps. No congregation can undertake all of these steps, and certainly not all at once. Each congregation should select those action steps that will work best for its local situation. But do not delay! The need for action is now.

INTERFAITH EFFORTS BY LOCAL COMMUNITIES AND CONGREGATIONS

Any congregation that heeds this call to become engaged will not be the first to do so. The following are some examples of interreligious and interracial endeavors that are already up and running. We cite them in order to stimulate ideas about what can be done and to offer encouragement that something is possible.

Large numbers of local projects are taking place, with people of several religions making them happen. Food banks and similar endeavors enjoy multireligious support. Joint Christian-Jewish-Muslim Thanksgiving Day services occur in many communities. In many states, an interreligious council works with the state legislature and governor to pass legislation of benefit to the entire community—in areas such as public assistance programs, protection of the environment, health care, prison reform, and antitrafficking efforts. A large number of educational endeavors help churches learn about their neighbors who practice other religions. There are also instances of shared parking lots, shared buildings, and even shared facilities for worship. The public demonstrations against the 2017 travel ban and against family separation at the southern border have usually been multireligious.

Remarkable stories of support for people of other faiths have emerged from these local initiatives. In early 2019 in Louisville, Kentucky, a Hindu temple was vandalized by a seventeen-year-old male who used spray paint to deface images of Hindu gods. On a subsequent Saturday, hundreds of local residents mobilized to help clean and restore the temple. As one commentator stated, "Though the perpetrator hoped to divide the community, the response helped unite people across ethnic, political, and religious lines."[1]

Recent events in our home state of Minnesota highlight very hopeful signs of people beginning to embrace religious diversity in our local communities. In Willmar, Minnesota, several congregations and local Muslims recently organized the Willmar Interfaith Network, using the motto of "We are better together." At a potluck organized by the network, attendees were asked to learn the names of at least two people they did not previously know, to hear the personal story of one of those people, and to share it with others. The community intends to continue this fruitful practice of hospitality and sharing. The network has also sponsored a two-day "Shoulder to Shoulder" training program, designed to enhance understanding of the Muslim faith and its practices.

In October of 2018 in Mankato, Minnesota, the First Congregational United Church of Christ hosted an interfaith gathering sponsored by six Christian congregations, the Mankato Islamic Center, Native American leaders, and the local Jewish community. Under the title of "Hope in a Time of Disruption," more than two hundred people gathered to share stories of difficult struggles encountered by recent immigrants as well as false understandings of religious beliefs and practices. At the same time, people spoke of the hope that comes from sharing each other's stories. One of the event organizers summarized the outcome in these words: "While the experiences discussed were painful, the communal gathering showed that people of different faiths and cultures can and are willing to listen to each other honestly and to search for a better way forward."[2] Similar interfaith gatherings have been held in recent years under the sponsorship of various churches and the Mankato Diversity Council.

In the state of Washington, the Reverend Terry Kyllo, an ELCA pastor, founded the Neighbors in Faith organization. Its mission is to educate congregations about Islam and to bring Muslims and Christians into neighborly relationships with each other. He and Muslim colleagues from the Muslim Association of Puget Sound have made presentations to hundreds of community, church, and education groups throughout the state. The program has strong support from regional ELCA synods and the area Episcopal Diocese, and it partners with the national Shoulder to Shoulder campaign.

Local faith groups, working with their local school districts, can often take the lead in facilitating a greater understanding of religious differences and respect for religious freedom. The school district of Modesto, California, like many midsized American communities, has seen a mix of religions emerge in its community. Evangelical megachurches are prominent in Modesto, along with Roman Catholic and more mainline Protestant churches and a sizeable Jewish community. In the last several decades, immigration has brought many people of other faiths to Modesto, including Buddhists, Sikhs, and Muslims. In response, the school district instituted a required course on world religions and religious liberty for all ninth graders. Surveys have indicated that the course has made a very positive difference in students' understanding of other religions and the importance of America's First Amendment right of religious liberty. It has also enhanced their personal daily interactions and their sharing of common moral values found in various faiths. An interfaith religious council helped create the course, hoping to avoid some of the problems and controversies that other communities have encountered when seeking to have religions taught in school. A local Baptist minister and member of the council spoke well for the group in saying, "We could find common ground because we all want kids to be safe."[3]

Encouraging signs of hope for interreligious understanding and mutual support are occurring not just among Christian groups but also among other faiths as well. Following the tragic shootings at the Tree of Life synagogue in Pittsburgh in October 2018, Muslim groups responded by raising two hundred thousand dollars to cover the cost of the funerals for the Jewish victims. This response happened because interfaith cooperation already existed. As reported at a gathering Darrell attended in December 2019, Jewish, Christian, and Muslim community leaders in Pittsburgh already had each other's phone numbers on speed dial. A San Francisco Sikh artist created 150 menorahs and then donated the profits to the local Jewish Community Relations Council.[4] During the time of the partial US government shutdown in January of 2019, volunteers from Islamic Circle of North America (ICNA), a national Muslim charity, assembled food bags at Logan Airport in Boston to distribute to families of airport workers who could not work because of the shutdown. During the deep freeze in Texas in February 2021, Muslim organizations in the state hosted warming stations and provided meals for thousands of cold and hungry Texans. Many other examples can be found throughout the country illustrating that people of all faiths can come together to help each other in times of need.

RACE-RELATED EFFORTS BY LOCAL COMMUNITIES AND CONGREGATIONS

For real progress to be made in racial matters in America, local churches and community groups are called to operate on two major fronts: (1) to cross racial lines and bring people together for dialogue and the sharing of thoughts, admissions of ignorance, and visions of hope for the future, and (2) to understand and to act to change the social and economic structures and policies that continue to prevent racial justice and obstruct equal opportunity for all Americans.

Numerous community organizations are working at fostering meaningful conversations among persons of different races. Local councils of churches are often deeply involved in these efforts. But for meaningful conversations to happen, people need to be enticed to move beyond their normal patterns of interaction. According to one estimate, 75 percent of white Americans, with the possible exception of their workplaces, have social circles that include only other white Americans.[5]

Communities are undertaking new ways to change patterns of interaction and bring people of different races together. In Columbia, Maryland, a Lutheran pastor, Rev. Ginny Price, teamed up with

Steven Lewis, an African American she met at a local exercise gym, to create a new way for people of color, whites, and the local police to come together. Using the gym as the organizational mechanism, they created Come-Unity, bringing people together bimonthly to discuss issues of racism, white privilege, racial healing, and reactions to current events. They have added outdoor fun and games to the mix as well. Rev. Price, the "gym pastor," describes the outcome to date as follows: "Meeting people where they are at the gym, discovering and sharing God's love, exercising physical and spiritual muscles, has produced much fruit in unexpected ways and places."[6]

Our home state of Minnesota provides a good example of the special need to develop more opportunities for people to cross racial lines and share personal stories and feelings. Recently, the Minnesota Historical Society Press produced an insightful book entitled *A Good Time for the Truth*. Edited by Sun Yung Shin, the book is a collection of essays and poems exploring race relations in Minnesota. An article entitled "People like Us" by David Lawrence Grant, who has advised the Minnesota Supreme Court on critical racial matters, is especially stimulating in challenging Minnesotans to understand much better what needs be done to embrace the growing racial diversity in the state, including people who are "not like us." The state is noted for its overall friendly and welcoming attitude, often characterized as "Minnesota Nice." The author observes that Minnesotans are quick to be nice to and help new arrivals get started but then expect them to be "self-sufficient" and do just fine, leaving them alone rather than continuing fellowship and ongoing dialogue. Grant calls on Minnesotans to spend much more time sharing their stories and seeking to understand, appreciate, and value such stories. "If you fail to value a people's stories," he says, "you fail to value them." At the same time, he holds out hope for real change: "We can listen—really listen—to one another's stories and learn from them. Collectively, we can learn to tell a story that includes *all* our stories . . . fashion a mosaic-like group portrait from those stories that we all can agree truly does resemble people like us."[7]

Mankato, Minnesota, is one community that is taking seriously the challenge to create opportunities for the sharing of stories across racial and ethnic lines. Under the leadership of the YWCA, an annual "It's Time to Talk" event has been created, with strong community-wide support. A recent event—with Sun Yung Shin, the author/editor noted above, as the headline speaker—brought together more than five hundred people who sat around tables to "reflect honestly on the role race plays in their lives." They heard "frank observations about the day-to-day experiences people of color face that white people don't." Reflecting the recent and fairly rapid growth of diversity in the city, one attendee remarked, "We need to at least talk about what's right in front of us, and that we are diverse. By sharing stories, I believe that it creates more empathy, understanding, and we can be more productive as a society."[8]

The nearby community of St. James, Minnesota, has created its own special way of bringing people of different races and cultural backgrounds together. Seeking to improve relationships among the longer-term residents of the area and the newer immigrants, who are primarily Hispanic, members of various churches organized a celebration of "culture through cuisine" with the sharing of Scandinavian and Latino foods. The groups then decided to continue annually with a "Multicultural Fiesta," now in its third successful year.

In our hometown of St. Peter, Minnesota, several churches of varying denominations have sponsored discussions on racism, interreligious dialogue, and initiatives for social justice. An interracial and interreligious group of local citizens has created the St. Peter Good Neighbor Diversity Council.

But dialogue and storytelling aimed at improving race relations are not enough to bring about true racial justice and racial equality in our America. The difficulty is that so many of the inequities are products of social structures and policies that have the effect of advantaging one group and disadvantaging another. All of the numerous efforts to bring people of diverse racial backgrounds into closer relationship and better understanding are but a necessary prelude to revising those social structures. Congregations are beginning to recognize their role in tackling these matters related to structure and policy. Mission committees are focusing not just on highway cleanup projects but also on the "cleanup" of policies that prevent racial progress and equality.

Bias and racial profiling often occur in local communities, but our local communities can also be the scene of important changes. The Nextdoor website that provides hundreds of local communities with announcements, community-building information, and warnings for safety discovered that racial profiling was taking place, especially in the reporting of "suspicious activity." The leaders of the website, after seeking outside review and advice, took action that included developing a checklist for describing suspicious people in the neighborhood that focused on behavior, not color, and called for careful, full descriptions of what was happening. As a result, racial profiling decreased by 75 percent.[9]

Signs of hope are also occurring as people have mobilized to give increasing public attention to the issue of mass incarceration and the disproportional numbers of people of color who receive prison sentences. In some communities, this awareness of the problem has led to the creation of restorative justice programs as an alternative to courtroom trials and sentencing. Local groups, including congregational social action committees, have also brought increased attention to the role of implicit and overt bias within some police departments that results in disproportional shooting deaths and police stops for people of color, and they have focused on taking action to overcome achievement disparities in public schools. Change is not easy, but real change is possible when people of faith, informed by the gospel call to love our neighbors—without exception—come together to talk, pray, and act.

And let us be honest about our current political situation. Bringing about changes in social and economic structures at this point in our history seems extremely difficult. Our federal government, reflecting the deep political divisions in our country, is currently too often dysfunctional. Legislative action to increase racial equality and improved educational and economic opportunities for all will not easily happen. The racism embedded in our current immigration practices will get corrected only with a major new immigration policy, but without more unified support, political leaders are reluctant to undertake this much-needed task.

Martin Luther King Jr. faced a similar situation at the beginning of the civil rights movement. Politicians were unwilling to act to overcome segregation and long-standing, racist Jim Crow laws. What made them change? Ordinary people, acting at the local level through churches and community organizations, prompted them to come on board. People of all colors, faiths, and economic statuses came together to demand that politicians act for the good of the country. Author Josina Guess recently visited the relatively new Mississippi Civil Rights Museum in Jackson. As she walked through the museum and saw the realistic and often difficult-to-observe exhibits from the past, she was discouraged, recognizing that racism, hate crimes, and structural inequality still exist today in America. At the same time, she became hopeful: "I felt gratitude for the museum's emphasis on the ordinary people, student groups, and churches, who had organized and resisted to the point of exile and death. It was clear that the movement was fueled by people of faith, which made me grieve how many churches were—and are— silent or complicit in government-sanctioned cruelty."[10]

FROM THE LOCAL TO THE NATIONAL

In order to tackle a societal problem such as racism or anti-Semitism or antipathy to the presence of other religions, larger coalitions are necessary. Though seldom reported in the public media, thousands of ongoing actions by Americans bring people together for dialogue, increased understanding, and cooperation. Actions are occurring at all levels of our society, including national ecumenical organizations, religious denominations, colleges and universities, and theological seminaries. Leaders of these organizations are helping to lead the way and inspire people at all levels of society to do their part in embracing religious and racial diversity. We will highlight a few of these efforts, both as a source of encouragement and as a possible avenue of collaboration.

CHRISTIAN ECUMENICAL MOVEMENTS

All the mainline Protestant churches that belong to the National Council of Churches (NCC) are involved in interreligious relations. Dialogues are underway in which representatives of the NCC meet regularly for bilateral conversations with Jews, Muslims, Buddhists, and Hindus. The separate dialogues are places not only to learn about the other religions but also to form networks of friendship and to seek areas of cooperation. The bilateral dialogues all come together at the NCC's interreligious "convening table."

A beautiful example of such "friendship" networks occurred when the Christian-Jewish dialogue group sponsored by the National Council of Churches* and the National Council of Synagogues met October 29–30, 2018. This was only about a week after the murders at the Tree of Life Synagogue in Pittsburgh. On October 30, the group assembled for a joint memorial service. As part of the service, Rabbi David Straus spoke. He talked about all four of his grandparents who lived in Germany on Kristallnacht (November 1938). Each pair watched from across the street as a synagogue was burned during the Nazi-inspired night of anti-Jewish destruction. They felt utterly alone. Their neighbors were either "outside cheering or inside their homes, looking the other way with curtains closed." By contrast, Rabbi Straus said, after the tragedy in Pittsburgh, his phone did not stop ringing, and the emails and texts kept coming, expressing horror, showing solidarity, and offering to help. They came from Christian partners, Muslims, and other citizens. Rabbi Straus stated, "It's not that hate and violence and anti-Semitism and racism are gone 80 years later, but we are not alone"[11] when people of faith and no faith stand together. For this, he expressed his gratitude. The tragic shooting killed more Jews than any other event in American history, but others stood with the survivors. Standing together across racial or religious lines has special importance at times of crisis or in the face of new threats.

---

* Darrell is a member of this dialogue group.

The National Council of Churches has also given leadership to creating the Shoulder to Shoulder campaign, founded in 2010 to actively improve relationships with American Muslims. Thirty-four national religious organizations have joined together to "work with congregations and communities across the nation to stand in multifaith solidarity with our Muslim neighbors."[12] The Shoulder to Shoulder campaign helps shatter false beliefs about Muslims. During a two-day training session, I (Bill) was impressed with how Shoulder to Shoulder is seeking to equip faith leaders to address anti-Muslim bigotry in their home communities. For example, participants at the training session learned that documented sociological opinion studies have demonstrated that Muslims in the United States (along with Jews) have stronger yearnings for peaceful solutions to problems—and less reliance on violence—than mainline Christians, and especially evangelical Christians.

Improving race relations is another major emphasis of the National Council of Churches. The historically Black churches are well represented on the various task forces and at the annual gathering. Recent annual gatherings have given particular attention to the problem of mass incarceration and to church-supported reentry programs for prisoners returning to their home communities. The fall gathering in 2019 was held in Newport News, Virginia—where, in 1619, the ship arrived that carried the first Africans who were sold into slavery. Amid laments for the tragic history came a call to move beyond its harmful legacy.

ACTION BY CHRISTIAN DENOMINATIONS

Both Catholic and mainline Protestant congregations are also providing leadership for many efforts aimed at educating their members about matters of racial justice, promoting interfaith understanding, and linking with neighbors of other colors and religions. For example, The Episcopal Church actively encourages the creation of local "Beloved Communities" where "all people may experience dignity and abundant life and see themselves and others as beloved children of God."[13] Through the Episcopal Office of Ecumenical and Interreligious Relations, the church fosters both dialogue and joint activities with other Christian denominations and with people of other religions. The United Church of Christ (UCC) has passed resolutions at its General Synod gatherings to reinforce the church's commitment to reconciliation with Jewish and Muslim communities. Through its Justice and Peace Action Network, the UCC calls its members to learn about and take action in regard to critical racial justice issues.

The Evangelical Lutheran Church in America (ELCA) has also been very active in interreligious organizations and dialogue. It has created an Ecumenical and Interreligious Relations team to be in regular communication with its Full Communion partner Christian denominations and reach out to people of other faiths to give support and offer hospitality. The ELCA has representatives on all the interreligious dialogues sponsored by the NCC. In addition, it has a Consultative Panel on Lutheran-Jewish Relations and a Consultative Panel on Lutheran-Muslim Relations. ELCA presiding bishop Rev. Elizabeth Eaton has responded quickly and boldly to the tragic killings of people of other faiths, in the United States and abroad, and has provided strong leadership on matters of racial justice.

At the same time, many in the ELCA recognize that the denomination has a long way to go to make the changes necessary to embrace both religious and racial diversity. ELCA Black pastor Lenny Duncan, in his recent book *Dear Church*, has pointed out that the ELCA is currently the whitest major denomination in the USA. He is highly critical of a denomination that has been too complacent regarding the need to challenge built-in roadblocks in both church and society. Yet he believes that the ELCA, as a church of "grace people," can lead—at the national level and in local congregations—by taking seriously the gospel calls to preach, teach, listen, and then engage in serious actions to strive toward racial inclusion and racial justice.[14]

The ELCA, at its Churchwide Assembly in August 2019, adopted challenging resolutions that have profound implications for interfaith and interracial relationships for all its members:

- Through a "Declaration of Interreligious Commitment," members are challenged to understand the perspectives of people of other faiths and work with them for positive change and peace.
- Through a "Strategy toward Authentic Diversity in the ELCA," members are challenged to move toward greater diversity and inclusiveness.
- Through the "Declaration of the ELCA to People of African Descent," members are challenged to move from old positions of complicity and silence toward actively pursuing racial justice.
- Through its decision to become a sanctuary church denomination, members are challenged to uphold the ELCA's long-standing commitment to serve immigrants and refugees.
- Through a special resolution, members are challenged to support the visions and goals of the Poor People's Campaign.
- Through a special resolution, assembly members voted to commemorate June 17 as a day of repentance for the martyrdom of the Emanuel Nine—the nine people who were shot and killed June 17, 2015, at Mother Emanuel AME Church in Charleston, South Carolina.
- Through a special resolution condemning white supremacy, members are challenged to give attention to the structures and rhetoric that empower and fuel white supremacy and "to take to heart the teaching of Scriptures, so we may all be better equipped to speak boldly about the equal dignity of all persons in the eyes of God."

What about the white evangelical churches where large numbers of Americans are faithful members? Are there signs of hope and action among these churches? Yes, there are. For many years, conservative white evangelical churches, especially in the South, gave strong support to the institution of slavery and to Jim Crow laws. During the civil rights movement these churches either stood on the sidelines or directly opposed the changes that would lead to desegregation, voting rights, and equal protection under the law for all people. As a very positive sign in recent years, many of these churches, their denominations, and their journalistic voices have begun to speak out for racial justice and to apologize for their earlier stances and actions. For example, Mark Galli, who was at the time editor in chief of *Christianity Today* (CT), the major religious periodical for evangelicals, recently wrote the following statement about the publication's communications during the civil rights era: "In short, during this crucial era of American history, CT did not lead as much as reflect the moral ambiguity and confusion of that era's white evangelical churches. Though today we champion racial justice as a vital component of Christian discipleship, we must acknowledge and repent of this part of our history."[15]

New perspectives in recent writings by devoted evangelical Christians have challenged fellow evangelicals. The late Douglas Miller, who served as a Baptist minister and Baptist seminary professor, recently authored a powerful book. It addresses directly what he sees as the misuse of American Christianity to justify injustice and to support self-serving political, cultural, religious, and social beliefs. The book, entitled *Your Jesus Is Too Small*, was completed just before Miller died from his courageous battle with cancer. He decries the fact that so many of his evangelical Christian friends and colleagues have "cast their lot on the political right," named the "Religious Right" by many. He was also concerned that some on the far left of the political spectrum too often proclaim that only their views can be seen as holy and ethical. Instead of clinging to a Jesus who is too "small," Miller calls us to follow the teachings of the real Jesus, the Jesus who is loving, compassionate, neighbor-serving, justice-minded, forgiving, truth-seeking, peace-loving, and character-transforming.[16] Doug Miller was more than a writer. He exemplified Jesus's call to action by giving leadership to important ecumenical and multiracial efforts in Southern California, especially to improve the lives of low-income and homeless people.

Another courageous and compelling testimony comes from Rev. Jonathan Wilson-Hartgrove in his book *Reconstructing the Gospel*, subtitled *Finding Freedom from Slaveholder Religion*. Wilson-Hartgrove grew up and was educated in a deeply conservative, evangelical environment, but living and serving as a pastor in a Black community in North Carolina revealed to him the racism that was embedded in much of what he was taught and took for granted. His call to fellow evangelicals to seek to undo the injustices of the past and reconstruct the gospel to bring good news to all is a call to all Christians, no matter what their theological backgrounds are.[17]

On Ash Wednesday 2018, a group of leaders from a wide variety of mainline denominations and Black churches and progressive members of evangelical denominations came together out of deep concern that "the soul of the nation and the integrity of faith are now at stake." Under the leadership of Rev. Michael Curry, presiding bishop of the Episcopal Church; Rev. Jim Wallis, president and founder of Sojourners; and others, they developed and issued a important "Reclaiming Jesus" statement. The statement rejects the "resurgence of white nationalism and racism in our nation" and proclaims that "racial justice and healing" are "central to the mission of the body of Christ in the world." They pledged to continue to send their message of love and reconciliation to "pastors, local churches, and young people who are watching and waiting to see what the churches will say and do at such times as these."[18]

EFFORTS AMONG COLLEGES AND UNIVERSITIES

Higher education is another area in which efforts are underway to enhance interreligious understanding. A major influence with college students has been the Interfaith Youth Corps (IFYC), started and overseen by Eboo Patel, an American-born Muslim. The goal of the IFYC is to work with higher educational institutions "to create high-quality, sustainable interfaith programming at every level of a college campus." Patel is convinced that "arrangements promoted by a college have a profound impact on the broader American society," and they help to "nurture a society's future leaders." He notes also that church-related colleges play a special role when he states that "because so many colleges in the United States were established by faith communities and welcome diversity, they also have an opportunity to model how to retain particularity while achieving pluralism."[19]

Many colleges have undertaken their own special programs to foster interreligious dialogue and understanding. One example at a church-related college is the Micah House at Augustana College in Rock Island, Illinois. Centered around the well-known biblical passage of Micah 6:8 ("What does the Lord require of you but to do justice, and to love kindness, and to walk humbly with your God?"), the house is home to a group of senior students who live "with the intention of growing in their faith together and serving the community in which they live." Over the years, Lutherans, Muslims, Catholics, Buddhists, and representatives of other faiths have come together for meals, sponsored interfaith dialogues for the broader campus community, and carried out service projects in the Rock Island / Moline area.[20]

Quite a different undertaking is the Pluralism Project, begun and led by Diana Eck at Harvard Divinity School. This project has mapped religious diversity in the United States for more than twenty-five years. By "religious pluralism," the project means something more than the mere existence of religious diversity. Pluralism goes beyond tolerance; it involves an active engagement that seeks understanding across lines of difference.[21] With this understanding of "pluralism," we concur.

Virtually every college or university in the country has programs that focus on improved racial relations. Because they see the value of racial and ethnic—as well as religious—diversity, they recruit students of various racial and ethnic backgrounds. They offer courses and organize student programs aimed at increasing interracial understanding. This commitment to racial diversity is occurring not just among colleges that are predominantly white but among institutions that have been mainly serving students of color as well. For example, Tennessee State University (TSU) in Nashville, Tennessee, one of the largest historically Black universities in America, has in recent years significantly increased its enrollment of white and Hispanic students. This increase reflects its strong commitment to serve the higher education needs of many students in Tennessee and beyond through its well-established programs.[*]

A special example for understanding Native American culture is found at Augustana University in Sioux Falls, South Dakota. In the 1980s, the institution not only recruited Native American students from the reservations in the state; it also periodically brought parents from the reservations to develop a sense of trust concerning the educational experiences their sons and daughters were receiving.[†] And for decades, the Campus Ministry at Augustana has organized a fall break learning experience on the Pine Ridge reservation in western South Dakota, where white students become the "racial minority" while receiving special lessons about the history and culture of the Lakota. The highly visible Center for Western Studies on the campus also highlights Native American culture, especially that of the Northern Plains, through exhibits and educational workshops for students and the general public.

LEADERSHIP FROM THEOLOGICAL SEMINARIES

Denominational and independent theological seminaries are also giving leadership to embracing the increasing religious diversity in America. Many seminaries are offering classes in interreligious understanding, and some host special institutes that operate both on and off campus. Institutes for Muslim-Christian relations, for

---

[*] In 2012, Bill served as the interim vice president for University Relations and Advancement at Tennessee State University.

[†] From 1980 to 1986, Bill served as president of Augustana College (now Augustana University).

example, can be found at Hartford Seminary in Connecticut, Luther Seminary in St. Paul, the Lutheran School of Theology in Chicago, and many others. Harvard Divinity School trains Buddhist spiritual leaders through its Buddhist Ministry Initiative. And Claremont School of Theology offers a graduate degree in Hebrew Bible and Jewish Studies.

Union Theological Seminary in New York City now offers Masters of Divinity programs in Christian Ministerial Leadership, Anglican Studies (in affiliation with Episcopal Divinity School at Union), Buddhism and Interreligious Engagement, and Islam and Interreligious Engagement. Muslim student Mohammad Mia said of the new Islam program, "What I have received at Union has been a space to engage in critical questions surrounding religious differences, religious plurality, and what it means to live a life informed by faith."[22]

Both Protestant and Catholic seminaries have also worked hard in recent years to increase racial diversity among students and faculty and help educate students and the denominations they serve concerning matters of racial equality and justice. Moreover, a very promising sign of hope for racial justice matters involves changes emerging among seminaries for evangelical denominations. For example, Southern Baptist Theological Seminary in Louisville, Kentucky, with the largest MDiv enrollment in the nation, recently issued a large seventy-page report that detailed its racial history, including the years of the institution's ties to slavery and claims of white superiority. In recent years, however, Southern has brought greater diversity to its faculty and student body. In the words of Marshal Ausberry, president of the Southern Baptist Church's National African American Fellowship—representing more than four thousand predominantly Black congregations—"Southern's transparency does not change the past but can move the seminary to a better future."[23]

Over the coming years, this leadership from ecumenical institutions, denominations, colleges, universities, and seminaries will continue to encourage the understanding and embracing of religious and racial diversity in America.

LIVING AND ACTING IN HOPE

With the predictions cited earlier that white Americans will in a few decades no longer be a majority but will be one minority among other minorities, the difficult question we face is this: How will Americans handle this transition? Will the change occasion chaos and conflict or an expanded sense of who is included? Current reactions to the growing racial and religious diversity and current responses to immigration seem to indicate a deep level of fear at work in American society. Can this fear be overcome? We return, once more, to hope.

Americans have traditionally been what Douglas John Hall calls "officially optimistic." This optimism looks around, sees things going well, and expects progress to continue. But this optimism has been pummeled by events of the twentieth century, including two world wars, several genocides, a cold war, the mushroom-shaped cloud, the silent spring, a new awareness of limited resources, and the like. What is needed now, amid fading optimism, is hope—the kind that exists even in the midst of darkness. Optimism does not lead to engagement; hope does. This hope reduces fear, overcomes the paralysis produced by global-sized problems, and equips us to be engaged in incremental change. The most important and most basic source of this hope is the message that God is at work in the world, behind the scenes, working in and through people to achieve a more just world.

Another source of hope is the resilience of American democracy. An appreciation of the past can inspire hope for the future. The process of change has not always been smooth, but our democracy has so far muddled its way through crisis after crisis. Our democracy also provides a legal framework that is tested with each new generation but continues to provide guidance, strength of purpose, and vision. While racial equality is yet to be realized, it is still a stated desire, and laws against discrimination continue to be strengthened. While courts sort out the exact details, they continue to provide a good degree of protection for religious freedom in our country.

The really good news about our democracy and our Bill of Rights is that we Americans have the freedom to act to bring about change. This is how progress has been made in America. What we Americans need to avoid is allowing our anxieties and fears to lead us to believe there are only two possibilities—to give in or to fight—rather than exploring the positive options that arise from the biblical view of wholeness and the responsibilities of citizenship. What we also need to avoid is allowing our anxieties and fears to settle only for a quick fix, strong-armed into place. This is the recipe for a disastrous unraveling of our nation's "grand experiment."

In the face of structural racism, both persons of color and those who are white need to assist, stand with, and stand up for those disadvantaged by the color lines. They will need to do this even when it brings no direct benefit to themselves. In the face of discrimination against and fear of people of other faiths, we need to learn from each other and come forward to help in times of need. Our focus needs to be on the future—a future that can bring a healthier community and a fuller, deeper humanity for all of our grandchildren.

The church, if faithful to its call, is itself a God-centered source of hope. The church can play a vital role in creating the support networks that move us forward. As it does so, it can welcome people of every background to join the effort. This effort will require cooperation, persistence, courage, and wisdom. Whatever people do to foster those qualities will be valuable. Every step offers a new reason to be encouraged. Every step can bring us closer to embracing our diversity and loving our neighbor—without exception.

CHAPTER EIGHT

Finding Joy in Diversity

When my (Bill's) family comes together around an enlarged holiday dinner table or at a family reunion, its three generations are glad for the opportunity to replace long-distance calling or texting with face-to-face conversation. Without necessarily expressing the feeling in words, we also find joy in experiencing wonderful combinations of both diversity and oneness. Our family includes Caucasians with DNA roots stretching from Scandinavia and Great Britain to southern Europe, African American and multiracial young adults, and people of Christian and Jewish faith commitments. Yet we are one family. We rejoice in this diversity, not out of a sense of pride, but out of a deep feeling that this is the way the world should be.

I (Bill) also recall other times when diversity produced a special sense of inner joy. When I was in Alabama in the spring of 1965, as a "foot soldier" for Martin Luther King Jr. and the Southern Christian Leadership Conference, I had the privilege of serving side by side with people of other races and religions. We faced danger together, but we also found great joy in holding hands and singing together the lively songs of the civil rights movement.

In the 1980s, about the time that I (Darrell) was organizing the Institute for Jewish-Christian Understanding, my twelve-year-old son had an extended stay in the hospital while he underwent three very serious abdominal surgeries (and returned later for a fourth).

When the surgeon asked for volunteers to donate blood to be used in one of the surgeries, the very first person to volunteer was a Jewish woman who had served on the planning committee. And my son's favorite visitor was a Jewish engineer and businessman who had also served on that committee. Throughout that month, God was hearing prayers both from Jews and from Christians.

A little earlier, the rabbi with whom I team-taught accepted an invitation to move to a congregation in another state. He invited me to participate in his installation service, and I asked him what I should wear. My rabbi friend said, "I want you to wear your ecclesiastical vestments." I wondered about this because my stole bore specifically Christian symbols—some of which could remind members of his new congregation of mistreatment at the hands of Christians. In another conversation, I asked again. The answer was the same. The day came for the service. Three or four neighboring rabbis and I participated—in my case, by reading part of the liturgy. At the end of the service, my rabbi friend spoke. And one of his remarks was how happy he was to have his "spiritual brother Darrell" participate. This gracious statement was deeply meaningful on its own terms. But as I thought about it, I also came to see that my friend had welcomed me into his sacred space just as I was, without having to leave any part of my religious identity at the door. For me, this is what asking me to wear ecclesiastical vestments signified. It was an act of profound interreligious hospitality.

LOVE, JOY, AND RELEASE FROM THE OLD ORDER

The Bible often speaks of joy as an outcome of God's purposes for us on this earth. In the midst of Jesus's final instructions to his disciples on the night of the Last Supper, he gives his new commandment to love one another and his wish that his people might "all be one." And he makes clear that he is giving all these instructions so that our "joy may be complete" (John 15:11). The apostle Paul in Romans 14:17 proclaims that the kingdom of God is "righteousness and peace and joy." Paul also reminds us that joy is a vital part of "the fruit of the Spirit" (Gal 5:22).

How do God's people move toward this feeling of greater joy? The noted biblical scholar Walter Brueggemann—in perhaps his most famous book, *The Prophetic Imagination*—describes how joy comes when people are released from the "old order," when all who are in the majority are no longer "numbed" by the expectation that it is OK to discriminate against certain people and keep them down. There is joy for everyone in this sense of newness when all people can come together, "released from the old order." This new way of people relating to each other is what the kingdom of God here on earth is all about! In Brueggemann's words, "Jesus' concern was, finally, for the joy of the Kingdom. That is what he promised and to that he invited people."[1]

FROM TOLERANCE AND APPRECIATION TO JOY

To reach this vision of joy and to embrace the growing racial and religious diversity in America, people of faith admittedly have important steps to take. We believe those steps can be summarized as tolerance, followed by appreciation, and then the experience of real joy.

Tolerance of other's beliefs, even when we do not agree with them, is a good place to start. John D. Inazu of Washington University, St. Louis, in his insightful book *Confident Pluralism*, identifies this need for tolerance of others in our American constitutional heritage. He argues that "tolerance is the most important civic aspiration."[2] Does a posture of tolerance mean that a person simply accepts all the beliefs of people who think differently, look different from us, or have a different set of religious beliefs than we do? No. Could a caring person accept a viewpoint that called for violence among us? Of course not. But tolerance does mean that we Americans can learn to accept our genuinely healthy differences. Inazu summarizes his approach to "confident pluralism" this way: "Instead of the elusive goal of E Pluribus Unum, it suggests a more modest possibility—that we can live together in our 'many-ness.'"[3]

Our American constitutional background continues to call us to conduct our democracy with a sense of tolerance for varying viewpoints. We have indeed had our nasty battles of words and difficulties in achieving needed legislative compromises. But Dr. Inazu is hopeful of our ability to find common ground. As he observes, "One of the great successes of the American experiment has been the ability of its citizens to achieve a modest unity against great odds."[4]

Tolerance that provides a "modest unity" is a useful goal, but to embrace racial and religious diversity, we Americans must go beyond tolerance to *appreciation*—appreciation of what other racial groups and their special cultures and other religious groups and their spiritual insights have to offer. This openness to appreciate warmly the sharing of perspectives, new ideas, and ways to serve each other for the common good will also encourage people to come together more frequently and more meaningfully.

Our profound hope is that more and more Americans can move beyond tolerance and appreciation of our diversity to the experience of real *joy*. We would argue that to embrace our diversity and to find real joy in doing so requires us to be in each other's presence. We must make denominational pronouncements more meaningful by engaging in active person-to-person, group-to-group dialogue and fellowship and, when appropriate, joint worship experiences. The gospel call to love our neighbor is a call to build loving, supportive relationships. It is also a call to seek justice and to bring about the needed changes in social structures and policies. Presbyterian minister Carolyn Helsel uses these words: "Loving others means much more than not offending someone. Love requires something greater: to actually know that other person, to seek to know them, and to love them. Rather than simply avoiding offending another, love means actively finding out ways to love and care for them."[5] This combination of knowing, loving, and working together for societal justice is what will produce real and lasting joy.

Several years ago, two great figures of the world's current religious landscape, the Dalai Lama and Anglican Archbishop Desmond Tutu, came together in northern India for a full week of fellowship and dialogue. Their discussions, summarized in a memorable volume entitled *The Book of Joy*, were "about transcending our narrow definitions and finding love and compassion for all of humanity." They recognized differences in their two faiths, but they found an abundance of shared beliefs that would encourage love of neighbor and respect for others' traditions. In answer to the question of what must be done to combat so much intolerance and fanaticism in our society, the Dalai Lama responded, "Education and wider contact are really the only solutions."[6] At the end of their week together, they were filled with the goodness that came from sharing their faith expressions; they decided to make sure "joy" was in the title of the book filled with their insights and wisdom.

In today's America, people of faith have so much to gain by using both the power of the gospel message and the promises of our American democracy as compelling guides to challenge us and help us embrace our diversity. Bringing people together, rejoicing in diversity, and overcoming fears and uncertainties will lead to a more peaceful, enjoyable, and uplifting situation for all of us.

Many fear diversity, often because they have not experienced it. They sometimes, therefore, generate narrow, false impressions of people different from themselves. Can people of faith help others move from fear to joy in this diverse society? Yes; that is our calling.

Those of us who have been fortunate enough to experience diversity must be careful of developing our own false impressions of people who seem less welcoming of those who differ from them. We are all "neighbors." We need to listen to each other. Yes, we must continue to speak out about the wrongness of discrimination and hateful actions and words. But we must lead in a positive fashion as well. We must share our joy.

SHARING JOYFUL EXPERIENCES

Here is where our experiences of joy in diversity rise to great importance. Sharing stories of joyful experiences of dialogue, service, worship, and fellowship with people of other races and creeds may lead people from fear to fellowship, from opposition to openness, and from reticence to meaningful relationships. We who have experienced this joy do not want to put other people down; we want to lift them up. Sharing our experiences of joy is a much better way to encourage these positive life changes among people who have yet to embrace religious and racial diversity. Indeed, sharing our joy is an important and meaningful part of our Christian vocation.

The Wind River Reservation in Wyoming is geographically the largest Native American reservation in the United States. The land is shared by the Arapahoe and Shoshone tribes. Several years ago, I (Bill) and two professional colleagues, including one Black man, visited the reservation to help launch an experimental educational improvement project. As part of our orientation to the Native American culture of the reservation, we three visitors were invited to participate in a sweat lodge ceremony. Inside a tightly enclosed tent structure, approximately fifteen men and women gathered in a circle around a basin of very hot coals and rocks. Water was poured on the coals and rocks periodically to create the hot steam that quickly filled the tent. Most importantly, each person in the circle was invited to share thoughts with the group, prompted by the purpose of the visit by these "outsiders" or by recent happenings in individual lives. The words expressed around the circle included amazing combinations of Christian prayer to God or Jesus, Native American wisdom of human ties to Mother Earth, and hopes for good things to come from the educational project. The emotional outcomes visible among this diversity of people and their beautiful expressions of faith were delightful to behold. This scene can best be described as people relating to each other with a quiet sense of joy, respect, love, and hospitality.

Joy comes to us in a variety of ways. It can come in a quiet, serene way when diverse people gather for prayer and thoughts. It can come when people of differing colors and faiths sing in unison a rousing spirit-filled song. It can come when an inner sense of something warm and positive in life results from forming a new relationship across lines of race or religion. It can come when persons of differing races or religions work together to help someone in need. In any case, we believe the result is what God desires among his people.

Indeed, as together we pursue our quest to encourage people to embrace racial and religious diversity in our special country called America, let us not neglect to point to the joyful outcome that God wants us all to experience.

Conclusion

From the beginning of the planning and discussions for this book, we have been driven and inspired by two interlaced visions—a vision for America living up to its promises for liberty, equality, and inclusion, and a vision for the church living up to the challenges and hopes of the gospel and giving leadership to embrace racial and religious diversity in our country.

In the preceding chapters, we have sought to envision a church that

- takes seriously the biblical message to love God with all our heart, mind, and strength, and to love our neighbors without exception;
- actively seeks to be inclusive and welcoming to all;
- engages meaningfully and often with people of other religions;
- informs its members of the structural changes needed in our society to achieve equal opportunity and social justice;
- uses the power of thousands of congregations to become strong advocates for these necessary changes;
- sets positive examples for bringing people into honest conversations, respecting each other despite differences of opinion; and
- continuously offers a sense of hope that we can move from brokenness to bonding, from hurt to healing.

We have also sought to articulate a vision for America that

- encourages civil discourse;
- lives up to its promises of liberty and equality for all, not just for some;
- sees our increasing racial and religious diversity as positive and beneficial for our nation, not something to be feared;
- moves beyond expressions of white supremacy and racist tendencies to inclusiveness and a belief in the value of all human beings;
- replaces narrow thinking driven by notions of American and Christian nationalism, identity politics, tribal mindsets, and divisive media with open and meaningful dialogue to work together for the common good; and
- sets an example for the rest of the world, demonstrating how people of varying races and religions can live and work together and care for each other.

We recognize that the people of our nation are often filled with uncertainty and even fear of change. We have outlined the challenges to overcome.

At the same time, we are greatly encouraged by what we see happening in congregations and communities throughout our land. We see people in urban areas finding new ways to work together to build stronger interracial and interreligious communities. We also see rural Midwestern people, often assumed to be conservative and reluctant to change, welcoming people of other religions and other races into their communities. These folks have shown a readiness to learn about others, to reach out, to share in food and fellowship, and to dialogue. They are driven by the gospel lessons of faith, hope, and love, and by long-term traditions of serving others in times of need, helping with the neighbor's harvest when injury or illness strikes, and gathering with others to "build a barn." These same traditions that helped newcomers long ago are helping the newcomers of today.

In the process of researching, reading, observing, participating in community events, and writing this book, we have also learned much about ourselves. We have been reminded about our own shortcomings. Despite the fact that we both have had good friends of other races and religions for many years, we have often failed to be sensitive to the difficulties these friends face every day in places where they do not feel welcomed and affirmed. And we have not always been prepared to act boldly enough and with a sense of urgency to argue for and give leadership to the changes needed in our church and our society.

The word *embrace* has been prominent in our thinking and writing from the beginning. We envision a church and a nation that goes beyond toleration and even beyond appreciation of religious and racial diversity. We want people to actively embrace and find real joy in this diversity, in this new pluralistic society of America.

We love Eboo Patel's definition of pluralism that includes "respect for different identities, relationships between diverse communities, and a commitment to the common good." When people show respect for their neighbors of other races or religions, when they build supportive and caring relationships, and when they join with others to work for the common good, they are visibly and enthusiastically embracing diversity.

Recently, before the onset of the coronavirus, we observed a dialogue session among people of several races and religions. They were also people with strong and diverse opinions—conservative, liberal, right, left, moderate, and independent. At the end of the session, a conservative white man and a Black, more liberal woman came forward to give each other a hug. These two had different views about several matters, but they had begun to understand each other much better and found important common beliefs. Their act of warmth and kindness was a literal "embracing" of diversity.

A physical embrace will not be appropriate for certain dialogue sessions, for people of certain cultures, or for times when we face the potential of spreading a virus. But the idea of embracing our diversity—in mind, word, and deed—can work for everyone. As citizens, we do not need to agree on everything, but our race or our religion should not be a dividing line that gets in the way of seeking to understand and care for each other.

Embracing racial and religious diversity is a vision we—as individuals, as a church, and as a nation—can and should pursue. And for Christians, our vocational call to embrace diversity is driven each day by the message to love our neighbors without exception!

Acknowledgments

In the process of writing a book about religious and racial diversity, we intentionally sought feedback and guidance from people of diverse religious and racial backgrounds. And for a book inspired by scriptural wisdom and aimed at motivating and mobilizing people in local congregations, we sought feedback and guidance from experienced theological and congregational leaders. As a result, we are deeply grateful to the following people who took time to read and provide valuable commentary on our original manuscript: Dr. James Lyons, noted African American educator and former president of several highly diverse colleges and universities; Jocelyn Lyons, African American educator and spiritual direction counselor; Affey Sigat, member of the Islamic Mosque in St. Peter, Minnesota, youth counselor and coordinator of educational equity for our local school district; Rev. Alan Bray, former senior pastor of First Lutheran Church, St. Peter; Pei-loh Lo, former vice president of operations for Scholarship America and active member and former lay vice president of Trinity Lutheran Church, St. Peter; and Dr. Robin Steinke, president of Luther Seminary, St. Paul, Minnesota. Thanks to each of you for your valuable advice.

As we undertook this writing venture, we sought counsel from Black authors who have challenged both church and society on the questions of race and racism. We are thankful to Dr. Drew Hart, Black professor of theology at Messiah College and author of two provocative books on race and the Christian faith, for affirming that there is an important role for white authors to speak directly to predominantly white congregations, calling for the changes necessary to move toward justice and the embracing of diversity. Thank you, Drew, for your encouragement.

We are also grateful to our spouses, Jan Jodock and Margie Nelsen, for their continuing endorsement and support of this project and for their own reading of the manuscript and helpful comments. Bill's multiracial granddaughter, Alaiyah, also read parts of the manuscript, along with Bill's daughters, Shawna and Sarah, and son, Bill. Thank you for your active support.

For bringing this book to life—and the opportunity for the messages of the book to reach so many people in local congregations and communities—we are deeply indebted to Will Bergkamp, vice president, business development of 1517 Media, including its Fortress Press imprint. His guidance in relation to chapter organization and additional historical and theological references was especially helpful. We are also thankful for Scribe Inc. and Layne Johnson of Fortress Press and their teams for their dedicated copyediting and production work to bring this book into print. Thank you.

Finally, we are thankful for the partnership that developed between us throughout this project. This book arose from our discovering so many common beliefs, values, and visions for a better America. Writing a book as coauthors is not always an easy assignment, but throughout the process, our respect for what each of us could bring to the project and our sense of colleagueship never wavered.

About the Authors
Darrell Jodock and William Nelsen

We live just two blocks from each other in St. Peter, Minnesota. We are members of the same local congregation, Trinity Lutheran Church. We are both graduates of Lutheran colleges. Darrell is an alumnus of St. Olaf College, Northfield, Minnesota, and grew up in rural North Dakota. Bill is a graduate of Midland College (now Midland University) in Fremont, Nebraska, and grew up in small towns in the state of Oregon. We met each other while in graduate school, brought together by the Danforth Graduate Fellowship program—which was designed to identify and support persons who would prepare for a vocation in higher education.

Though linked by this fellowship program, our paths diverged. Darrell earned a seminary degree and a doctorate in historical theology. He pursued a teaching career that brought him to a Lutheran seminary and three Lutheran colleges. Bill earned a master's degree in religion and ethics and a doctorate in political science. He became a teacher and an academic dean at one Lutheran college and the president at another, president of a national scholarship organization, and—as a member of The Registry—an interim president or vice president at several other schools, including a seminary.

Our strong interest in racial diversity came from different pathways. Darrell was first exposed to critical racial issues as an intern and later as a pastor at a church in Washington, DC. More recently, his involvement in the National Council of Churches has given him access to leaders of traditionally Black churches and to other leaders in the ongoing struggle against racism. During the civil rights movement, Bill went south to Alabama, serving for a time under Rev. Martin Luther King Jr. and the Southern Christian Leadership Conference, and later spent three years as a "community lay minister" in an all-Black neighborhood in Philadelphia. More recently, he also served as an interim vice president at Tennessee State University, one of the nation's largest historically Black universities.

Our strong interest in religious diversity grew from differing experiences as well. Darrell became involved in Jewish-Christian relations while serving on the faculty of Muhlenberg College in Pennsylvania. There he founded the Institute for Jewish-Christian Understanding. More recently, he has chaired the ELCA Consultative Panel on Lutheran-Jewish Relations, has participated actively in two extended national Jewish-Christian dialogues—one on the Middle East and the other on pastoral issues—has participated in the Convening Table on Inter-Religious Relations of the National Council of Churches, has coauthored two books on interreligious relations, and has helped write "A Declaration of Inter-Religious Commitment" for the ELCA. Bill linked with people of various faiths initially as an international fellow at Columbia University. There he was selected for a United Nations internship program in Geneva, Switzerland, where he interacted daily with people of differing faiths from around the world. As part of his seminary education, he was involved in Muslim-Jewish-Christian interfaith dialogues in Israel and Palestine. More recently, he was selected for special leadership training for ethnically diverse communities, sponsored by the Blandin Foundation of Minnesota.

We arrived in the same neighborhood in St. Peter, Minnesota, for different professional reasons. Following his career at Muhlenberg College, Darrell came to serve as the first Drell and Adeline Bernhardson Distinguished Professor of Religion at Gustavus Adolphus College. Bill, following his time as a political science teacher and academic dean at St. Olaf College and president of Augustana University (SD), came to serve as president of Scholarship America, the nation's largest private-sector scholarship organization.

We both care deeply about the church and its future. Darrell has been a speaker and seminar leader in the church for many years, at local, synod, and national levels. He was ordained in 1973 and served a parish for two years before returning to teaching. Bill, active for many years in church-related higher education, returned to seminary at age sixty-four to become ordained in the ELCA and has served in local parishes and on the staff of the Southwestern Minnesota Synod. He was also called to serve as University Minister at his alma mater, Midland University, and as the Registry Interim President of Episcopal Divinity School in Massachusetts. We feel strongly that the church can and must play a prominent leadership role in fostering and embracing religious and racial diversity in America, and doing so, we believe, will strengthen the church's ability to carry out God's work in the future.

Notes

CHAPTER ONE

1 William H. Frey, *Diversity Explosion: How New Racial Demographics Are Remaking America* (Washington, DC: Brookings Institution Press, 2018), 1.
2 Frey, ix.
3 Frey, 5.
4 Frey, 249.
5 Frey, 3.
6 Frey, 6.
7 Pew Research Center, "America's Changing Religious Landscape," May 12, 2015, http://www.pewforum.org/2015/05/12/americas-changing-religious -landscape. References to the 2007–14 Pew comparative report come from this same source.
8 Pew Research Center, "In U.S., Decline of Christianity Continues at Rapid Pace," October 17, 2019, https://www.pewforum.org/2019/10/17/in-u-s -decline-of-christianity-continues-at-rapid-pace/.
9 Eboo Patel, *Out of Many Faiths: Religious Diversity and the American Promise* (Princeton, NJ: Princeton University Press, 2018), 9.
10 Patel, 20.

CHAPTER TWO

1 Clarence Jordan, *The Cotton Patch Version of Luke and Acts: Jesus' Doings and the Happenings* (New York: New Wind, 1969), 46–47.
2 Carol Schersten LaHurd, ed., *Engaging Others, Knowing Ourselves: A Lutheran Calling in a Multi-religious World* (Minneapolis: Lutheran University Press, 2016), 172.
3 C. S. Lewis, *Mere Christianity* (New York: Collier, 1952), 43.
4 As quoted in Benjamin Perry, "LaGrange and the Lynching Tree," *Union Collective*, Spring 2019, 4.

CHAPTER THREE

1 Gary Wills, as referenced in Jon Meacham, *The Soul of America: The Battle for Our Better Angels* (New York: Random House, 2018), 40.

2 Arthur M. Schlesinger Jr., as quoted in Meacham, *Soul of America*, 6.

3 Gunnar Myrdal, *An American Dilemma*, as referenced in Meacham, 6.

4 Meacham, 8.

5 For a description of these early abolition movements, see Paul J. Polgar, *Standard-Bearers of Equality: America's First Abolition Movement* (Chapel Hill: University of North Carolina Press, 2019).

6 Jemar Tisby, *The Color of Compromise* (Grand Rapids, MI: Zondervan, 2019), 102.

7 Richard Rothstein, *The Color of Law: A Forgotten History of How Our Government Segregated America* (New York: Liveright, 2017).

8 See Adam Cohen and Elizabeth Taylor, *American Pharaoh: Mayor Richard J. Daley: His Battle for Chicago and the Nation* (New York: Little, Brown, 2001).

9 Meacham, *Soul of America*, 82.

10 Meacham, 86.

CHAPTER FOUR

1 Jerry Spinelli, *Maniac Magee*, 25th anniv. ed. (New York: Little, Brown, 2015).

2 Rabbi Shai Held, "In Genesis 1, We're All Royalty: The Creation Story and the Divine Right of Everybody," *Christian Century*, November 7, 2018, 12.

3 Frey, *Diversity Explosion*, 10.

4 Jennifer Eberhardt, *Biased: Uncovering the Hidden Prejudice That Shapes What We See, Think, and Do* (New York: Penguin Random House, 2019), 6.

5 Eberhardt, 31–32.

6 Maria Godoy and Daniel Wood, "What Do Coronavirus Racial Disparities Look like State by State?," NPR, May 30, 2020, https://www.npr.org/sections/health-shots/2020/05/30/865413079/what-do-coronavirus-racial-disparities-look-like-state-by-state.

7 Jamil Smith, "Blackface Is Just One Part of the Problem," *Rolling Stone*, February 4, 2019, https://www.rollingstone.com/politics/politics-features/blackface-is-just-one-part-of-the-problem-789635/.

8 Sabrina Tavernise, "Why the Announcement of a Looming White Minority Makes Demographers Nervous," *New York Times*, November 22, 2018, https://www.nytimes.com/2018/11/22/us/white-americans-minority-population.html.

9 See reference to the Heartsong Church–Islamic Cultural Center story in Jim Wallis, *Christ in Crisis* (New York: HarperOne, 2019), 39–42. The description of the change of thinking by a member of Heartsong church

comes from a documentary entitled "Heartsong Church Welcomes Muslim Neighbors," Upworthy Video, YouTube: https://www.youtube.com/watch?v=kYembGqZF94.

10 Drew G. I. Hart, *Trouble I've Seen: Changing the Way the Church Views Racism* (Harrisonburg, VA: Herald, 2016), 176.

11 Hart, 59.

12 Hart, 67–68.

13 Richard Green, Registry internal document, September 2020.

14 Ibram X. Kendi, *How to Be an Antiracist* (New York: One World, 2019), 18.

15 Kendi, 22–23.

16 Eberhardt, *Biased*, 297.

17 Michelle Alexander, *The New Jim Crow: Mass Incarceration in the Age of Colorblindness* (New York: New Press, 2010).

18 Michelle Alexander, "Cruel and Unequal," *Sojourners*, February 2011, as quoted by Jim Wallis, *America's Original Sin: Racism, White Privilege, and the Bridge to a New America* (Grand Rapids, MI: Brazos, 2016), 158.

19 Alexander, *New Jim Crow*, 133.

20 Alexander, 133.

21 Eberhardt, *Biased*, 116.

22 Kendi, *Antiracist*, 238.

23 "Two Years after Travel Ban, Faith-Based Refugee Groups Struggle to Stay Open," *Christian Century*, April 10, 2019, 15.

24 Robert P. Jones, *The End of White Christian America* (New York: Simon & Schuster, 2016), 159.

25 Jason Micheli, "Can Christians Transform Culture?" *Christian Century*, August 29, 2018, 34.

26 Frey, *Diversity Explosion*, 31.

27 Jonathan Haidt, *The Righteous Mind* (New York: Vintage, 2012), 57–58.

28 Samantha Swindler, "As Sovereign Citizens Take the Mic at Hillsboro Grange, Community Leaders Sound an Alarm," *Oregonian*, December 7, 2018, https://www.oregonlive.com/news/2018/12/as-sovereign-citizens-take -the-mic-at-hillsboro-grange-community-leaders-sound-an-alarm.html.

29 Southern Poverty Law Center report, cited by Patel, *Out of Many Faiths*, 56.

30 Southern Poverty Law Center, *The Year in Hate and Extremism*, 2019 Annual Report, p. 4, https://www.splcenter.org/sites/default/files/yih_2020_final.pdf.

31 Editors, "Discrimination Is Community's Problem," *Mankato Free Press*, April 28, 2019, A4.

32 Cindy Wang Brandt, "Teaching Children about Racism," *Christian Century*, February 13, 2019, 26.

33 Eberhardt, *Biased*, 239.

34 Carolyn B. Helsel, *Anxious to Talk about It: Helping White Christians Talk Faithfully about Racism* (St. Louis: Chalice, 2017), 83.

35 See Will Herberg, *Protestant-Catholic-Jew: An Essay in American Religious Society* (Garden City, NY: Doubleday, 1955).

36 Eberhardt, *Biased*, 33.

37 Justin Lee, *Talking across the Divide: How to Communicate with People You Disagree with and Maybe Even Change the World* (New York: TarcherPerigee, 2018), 87.

38 Maria Ressa, "Facebook Let My Government Target Me but the Social-Media Giant Could Yet Fulfill Its Original Promise," *Time*, January 28, 2019, 31.

39 James Hankins, "The Forgotten Virtue: Humanitas Is the Cure for Incivility," *First Things*, December 2018, 33.

40 Michael Ignatieff, *The Ordinary Virtues: Moral Order in a Divided World* (Cambridge, MA: Harvard University Press, 2017), 51.

41 Patel, *Out of Many Faiths*, 13.

42 Francis Fukuyama, as quoted by Trey Popp, "Who Is America?," *Pennsylvania Gazette*, November/December 2018, 39.

43 Eleanor Roosevelt, as quoted by Judy Hinckley, "With Freedom Comes Responsibility," The Public Forum, The Salt Lake Tribune, St. Lake City, Utah, May 15, 2020, https://www.sltrib.com/opinion/letters/2020/05/15/letter-with-freedom-comes/.

44 Ed Stetzer, "How to Live with Religious Polarization," *USA Today*, November 9, 2015, 7A.

45 Martin Kaste, "I'm a Lutheran," *Living Lutheran*, April 2019, 12.

46 Jones, *White Christian America*, 236.

CHAPTER FIVE

1 See, for example, Graeme Wood, *The Way of the Strangers: Encounters with the Islamic State* (New York: Random House, 2017), 76, 146, 147, 268.

2 As reported by Julie Zauzmer, "The Alleged Shooter Was a Churchgoer Who Talked Christian Theology, Raising Tough Questions for Evangelical Pastors," *Washington Post*, May 1, 2019, https://www.washingtonpost.com/religion/2019/05/01/alleged-synagogue-shooter-was-churchgoer-who-articulated-christian-theology-prompting-tough-questions-evangelical-pastors/.

3 As reported by David Neiwert, "Hate Groups Are Recruiting Our Young People into a Toxic Belief System," CNN, May 4, 2019, https://www.cnn.com/2019/05/03/opinions/david-neiwert-white-nationalism-hate-groups-usoa/index.html.

4 Robert Bellah, "Civil Religion in America," *Daedalus: Journal of the American Academy of Arts and Sciences* 96 (Winter 1967): 1–21.

5 National Council of Churches, "The Dangers of Christian Nationalism in the United States: A Policy Statement of the National Council of Churches," April 20, 2021, https://nationalcouncilofchurches.us/common-witness-ncc/the-dangers-of-christian-nationalism-in-the-united-states-a-policy-statement-of-the-national-council-of-churches/. Darrell served on the task force that wrote this statement.

6 Laurent A. Parks Deloz et al., *Common Fire: Leading Lives of Commitment in a Complex World* (Boston: Beacon, 1996), 63.

7 Mustafa Akyol, as quoted by Jayson Casper, "Is ISIS Really Muslim?," *Christianity Today*, March 2019, 15.

8 "No Masses: Catholic Services Canceled in Sri Lanka," *Mankato Free Press*, April 27, 2019, A3.

9 Angela Denker, *Red State Christians: Understanding the Voters Who Elected Donald Trump* (Minneapolis: Fortress, 2019).

10 Bruce Feiler, *Where God Was Born: A Journey by Land to the Roots of Religion* (New York: HarperCollins, 2005), 372.

11 Feiler, 369.

12 Feiler, 376.

13 Robert Putnam and David Campbell, *American Grace: How Religion Divides and Unites Us* (New York: Simon & Schuster, 2010).

14 Alexis de Tocqueville, *Democracy in America*, tr. and ed. by Harvey C. Manfield and Delba Winthrop (Chicago: University of Chicago Press, 2000), 28.

15 Robert D. Putnam, *Bowling Alone: The Collapse and Revival of American Community* (New York: Simon & Schuster, 2012), 454, as referenced by Patel, *Out of Many Faiths*, 14.

16 Diana L. Eck, *A New Religious America: How a "Christian Country" Has Become the World's Most Religiously Diverse Nation* (New York: HarperSanFrancisco, 2001), 306.

17 Reza Aslan, *No God but God: The Origins, Evolution, and Future of Islam* (New York: Random House, 2005), 262.

18 Mustafa Khattab, trans., *The Clear Quran* (Lombard, IL: Book of Signs Foundation, 2016).

19 Eck, *A New Religious America*, 289.

20 Eck, 216.

21 Nitika Sharma, quoted in "Global Hindu Gathering Sparks Debate over Pride in Religious Identity," *Christian Century*, October 10, 2018, 13.

22 Davinder Singh, as quoted by Gary Worth, *Chicago Tribune*, "Sikh Couple Launches Drive to Help Feed Homeless," *Mankato Free Press*, November 18, 2018, E2.

23 Associated Press, "Kindness Comes One Slice of Pizza at a Time," *Mankato Free Press*, May 18, 2020, A2.

24 Ignatieff, *Ordinary Virtues*, 198.

25 Ignatieff, 19–20.

26 Kathleen A. Cahalan and Douglas J. Schuurman, *Calling in Today's World: Voices from Eight Faith Perspectives* (Grand Rapids, MI: William B. Eerdmans, 2016).

27 Interfaith Conference of Metropolitan Washington, Statement of Mission on ICMW website, https://ifmw.org.

28 Elizabeth A. Eaton et al., "ELCA Presiding Bishop, Faith Leaders Issue Statement on Children in Detention," *ELCA News*, June 6, 2019, https://www
.elca.org/News-and-Events/7982?_ga=2.188670432.930205495.1625759195
-475654678.1623789291. The statement was signed by representatives of the
Reformed Church of America, Islamic Relief USA, the African Methodist
Episcopal Zion Church, the United Methodist Church, the Episcopal Church,
the United Church of Christ, the Mennonite Church USA, the Christian
Church (Disciples of Christ), the Union of Reform Judaism, Churches Uniting
in Christ, Christian Churches Together, Moravian Church Northern Prov-
ince, the General Assembly of the Presbyterian Church, the Religious Action
Center of Reform Judaism, the Christian Methodist Episcopal Church, the
African Methodist Episcopal Church, the Islamic Society of North America,
the International Council of Community Churches, the National Council
of Churches of Christ in the USA, and the Evangelical Lutheran Church in
America.
29 Mall Area Religious Council, "About," https://www.facebook.com/
Mall-Area-ReligiousCouncil-111351098893384.
30 Interfaith Power and Light, "Mission Statement," https://www.interfaith
powerandlight.org/about/mission-history.

CHAPTER SIX

1 Deloz et al., *Common Fire*, 63.
2 Deloz et al., 67.
3 "We're All Royalty," *Christian Century*, November 7, 2018, 12.
4 Evangelical Lutheran Church in America, *A Declaration of Inter-religious
Commitment: A Policy Statement of the Evangelical Lutheran Church in
America*, August 8, 2019, https://download.elca.org/ELCA%20Resource
%20Repository/Inter-Religious_Policy_Statement.pdf?_ga=2.256683020
.62050339.1623789291-475654678.1623789291.
5 Martin Luther, "To the Councilmen of All Cities in Germany That They
Establish and Maintain Christian Schools," *Luther's Works: Christian in
Society II* (Philadelphia: Muhlenberg, 1962), 45:368–69.
6 Martin Luther, "Admonition to Peace: A Reply to the Twelve Articles of the
Peasants in Swabia," *Luther's Works: Christian in Society III* (Philadelphia:
Fortress, 1969), 46:19–23.
7 Rabbi Irving Greenberg in Eugene Fisher, ed., *Visions of the Other: Jewish and Christian Theologians Assess the Dialogue* (New York: Paulist,
1994), 8.
8 Putnam, *Bowling Alone*.

CHAPTER SEVEN

1 WHAS Newscast, February 2, 2019, as reported in *Christian Century*, February 27, 2019, 8.

2 Editors, "Local Faith Leaders Help Bring Different Cultures Together," *Mankato Free Press*, October 16, 2018, A4.

3 Emile Lester and Patrick S. Roberts, "How One School District Found Religion," *USA Today*, May 22, 2006, 13A.

4 "Anti-Semitic Incidents Persist Even as Jews Find Greater Acceptance," *Christian Century*, January 2, 2019, 16.

5 Robert P. Jones, "Self-Segregation: Why It's So Hard for Whites to Understand Ferguson," *Atlantic Monthly*, August 21, 2014, cited by Wallis, *America's Original Sin*, 199.

6 Erin Strybis, "The Gym Pastor," *Living Lutheran*, January 2019, 17.

7 David Lawrence Grant, "People like Us," in *A Good Time for the Truth: Race in Minnesota*, ed. Sun Yung Shin (St. Paul: Minnesota Historical Society Press, 2016), 209, 212.

8 Brian Arola, "Time to Talk," *Mankato Free Press*, December 5, 2018, B1.

9 As reported in Eberhardt, *Biased*, 185–86.

10 Josina Guess, "Reckoning with Racism," *Christian Century*, January 16, 2019, 25.

11 The quotations from Rabbi Straus have been confirmed via private correspondence with him.

12 "Our Partners," Home, Shoulder to Shoulder, November 15, 2019, http://www.shouldertoshouldercampaign.org.

13 Lenny Duncan, *Dear Church: A Love Letter from a Black Preacher to the Whitest Denomination in the US* (Minneapolis: Fortress, 2019).

14 The Episcopal Church, "Becoming Beloved Community: Vision," https://www.episcopalchurch.org/belovedcommunity/.

15 Mark Galli, "Where We Stand," *Christianity Today*, December 2018, 28.

16 Douglas J. Miller, *Your Jesus Is Too Small: The Collapse of Christian Character* (Eugene, OR: Cascade, 2018).

17 Jonathan Wilson-Hartgrove, *Reconstructing the Gospel: Finding Freedom from Slaveholder Religion* (Downers Grove, IL: IVP, 2018).

18 "Lent 2020: A Call to Prayer, Fasting, and Repentance Leading to Action," Reclaiming Jesus, May 31, 2018, http://www.reclaimingjesus.org.

19 Patel, *Out of Many Faiths*, 29.

20 Cindy Uke, "One House, Many Religious Expressions," *Living Lutheran*, November 2018, 44–46.

21 Eck, *A New Religious America*, 17–25.

22 *Union Collective*, Spring 2019, 13.

23 Marshal Ausberry, "Southern's Exposure," *Christianity Today*, April 2019, 13–15.

CHAPTER EIGHT

1 Walter Brueggemann, *The Prophetic Imagination*, 2nd ed. (Minneapolis: Fortress, 2001), 118.
2 John D. Inazu, *Confident Pluralism: Surviving and Thriving through Deep Difference* (Chicago: University of Chicago Press, 2016), 87.
3 Inazu, 6.
4 Inazu, 149.
5 Helsel, *Anxious*, 35.
6 Dalai Lama and Desmond Tutu, *The Book of Joy: Lasting Happiness in a Changing World* (New York: Avery, 2016), 71.